I0104728

Enhancing Public Accountability in Spain Through Continuous Supervision

))OECD

BETTER POLICIES FOR BETTER LIVES

The project was co-funded by the European Union via the Structural Reform Support Programme (REFORM/ IM2020/006). This publication was produced with the financial assistance of the European Union. The views expressed herein can in no way be taken to reflect the official opinion of the European Union.

This document, as well as any data and map included herein, are without prejudice to the status of or sovereignty over any territory, to the delimitation of international frontiers and boundaries and to the name of any territory, city or area.

Please cite this publication as:
OECD (2021), *Enhancing Public Accountability in Spain Through Continuous Supervision*, OECD Public Governance Reviews, OECD Publishing, Paris, *https://doi.org/10.1787/825740cc-en*.

ISBN 978-92-64-39505-3 (print)
ISBN 978-92-64-73404-3 (pdf)

OECD Public Governance Reviews
ISSN 2219-0406 (print)
ISSN 2219-0414 (online)

Photo credits: Cover image © Maria Savenko/Shutterstock and Gearings image © OECD, designed by Christophe Brilhault.

Foreword

Public administration reform has been a top priority for the government in Spain for the last decade. Following the establishment of the Commission for the Reform of the Public Administration (*Comisión para la Reforma de la Administración*, CORA) in 2012, reforms have accelerated, with the aim of strengthening the ability of government entities to deliver high-quality services to citizens and businesses, while enhancing transparency and accountability. Several key reforms focussed on the General Comptroller of the State Administration (*Intervención General de la Administración del Estado*, IGAE) and the National Audit Office (*Oficina Nacional de Auditoría*, ONA). One gave these entities a mandate to design a continuous supervision system (*sistema de supervisión continua*, SSC), administered by the ONA.

Through the SSC, the ONA seeks to improve the independent scrutiny and evaluation of public policies by monitoring risks associated with government entities' compliance with laws and regulations, financial sustainability and relevance. Ultimately, the SSC is meant to enhance accountability of the government to taxpayers. As Spain recovers from the COVID-19 pandemic, and advances with its Recovery, Transformation and Resilience Plan for 2021 to 2026, having effective control and supervision mechanisms in place is timely and critical.

This report discusses the SSC and the ONA's progress in the early stages of its implementation. Overall, the ONA has responded quickly and effectively to implement an approach to continuous supervision that is tailored to the Spanish context. It now faces the challenge of improving on its early progress, and iterating new versions of the SSC that exceed the high bar it has set for itself. This report offers considerations and recommendation for the ONA as it develops the SSC further. It focuses on ways for the ONA to strengthen its risk-based approach, enhance its strategy and capacity for data-driven monitoring and improve the ways it communicates and co-ordinated with government stakeholders to promote transparency.

This project was carried out with funding from the European Union via the Structural Reform Support Programme and in co-operation with the European Commission's DG Structural Reform Support. This document was approved by the OECD Working Party of Senior Public Integrity Officials (SPIO) on 01 November 2021and declassified by the Public Governance Committee on 23 November 2021. It was prepared for publication by the OECD Secretariat.

Acknowledgements

Under the direction of Elsa Pilichowski, OECD Director for Public Governance, and Julio Bacio Terracino, Acting Head of the Public Sector Integrity Division, this project was led by Gavin Ugale. Jael Billy wrote a first draft, and Frederic Boehm provided input and advice. Meral Gedik, Andrea Uhrhammer, Laura Völker and Elisabeth de Vega Alavedra provided editorial assistance. Charles Victor and Aman Johal provided administrative support, and Balazs Gyimesi contributed to communications and publication design.

The OECD is grateful to colleagues in the National Audit Office of Spain (*Oficina Nacional de Auditoría*, ONA) and the General Comptroller of the State Administration (*Intervención General de la Administración del Estado,* IGAE) for their fruitful co-operation and leadership. In particular, the OECD would like to thank Jorge Castejón González, Director of ONA, and his team, Álvaro Garnica Sainz De Los Terreros and Luis Miguel Jiménez Fernández. From the IGAE's Office of Budgetary Informatics, the OECD would also like to thank Ismael García Cebada, Chief of Division I, Accounting and Control Applications. Finally, the OECD is grateful to Ciresica Feyer of the European Commission's Directorate-General for Structural Reform Support (DG REFORM) for her guidance throughout the project and input on the draft report.

Table of contents

FIGURES

TABLES

Follow OECD Publications on:

http://twitter.com/OECD_Pubs

http://www.facebook.com/OECDPublications

http://www.linkedin.com/groups/OECD-Publications-4645871

http://www.youtube.com/oecdilibrary

http://www.oecd.org/oecddirect/

Abbreviations and acronyms

AIREF	the Independent Authority for Spanish Fiscal Responsibility
	La Autoridad Independiente de Responsabilidad Fiscal
CORA	Commission for the Reform of the Public Administration
	Comisión para la Reforma de la Administración
EA	Enterprise Architecture
EU	European Union
FMC	financial management control
HR	human resources
IA	internal audit
IBP	the International Budget Partnership
IGAE	The General Comptroller of the State Administration
	Intervención General de la Administración del Estado
IIA	the Institute of Internal Auditors
IMS	the Irregularities Management System
INVESPE	Inventory of Public Sector Entities
	Inventario de Entes del Sector Público
IPSASB	The International Public Sector Accounting Standards Board
ISA	International Standards on Auditing
ISSAI	the International Standards of the Supreme Audit Institutions
IT	Information Technology
NDPB	non-departmental public body
OIP	Office of Finance and Information Technology
	Oficina de Informática Presupuestaria
ONA	National Audit Office
	Oficina Nacional de Auditoría
ONC	Public Accounts Office
	Oficina Nacional de Contabilidad
PIFC	Public Internal Financial Control
SSC	continuous supervision system
	sistema de supervisión continua

Executive summary

Continuous supervision has developed over decades as a way for auditors to enhance their oversight of public funds. Approaches to continuous supervision vary, but, in general, it involves assessing risks and controls to help management determine the need for and nature of corrective actions or further inquiry. Continuous supervision complements traditional auditing by providing an early warning system to catch problems before they compound. It relies on reliable data and information technology systems to facilitate data collection and analysis.

In Spain, the contemporary origins for continuous supervision stem from nearly a decade of reforms to improve the efficiency of the public administration, increase its accountability and transparency and enhance public service delivery. In 2012, the Spanish national government established the Commission for the Reform of the Public Administration (CORA). At the time, the CORA 2013 reform package was one of the most substantial, evidenced-based and wide-ranging public governance reform plans among OECD member countries. The CORA recognised the strategic potential of information technology and digital tools to help achieve the proposed policy reforms, building on previous efforts at both the domestic and European levels.

One of the desired outcomes of the CORA reform package was an improved institutional architecture for the public sector. To achieve this, the CORA proposed regular monitoring and evaluation of the "rationality" of public sector entities in Spain with the goal of identifying those that could be dissolved or merged with others performing similar functions. The Public Administration Legal Regulation Act of 2015 (*Ley 40/2015 de 1 de octubre de Régimen Jurídico del Sector Público*) codified some of the CORA reform proposals to improve administrative efficiency, reduce duplication and simplify procedures across the public sector.

This Act also established the legal framework for a continuous supervision system for public sector entities (*sistema de supervisión continua*, SSC), spearheaded by the General Comptroller of the State Administration (*Intervención General de la Administración del Estado*, IGAE) and the National Audit Office (*Oficina Nacional de Auditoría*, ONA), the financial control and internal audit body within IGAE. In 2019, IGAE implemented its first iteration of the methodology for the SSC — an approach to independent evaluation of public policies with a focus on the entities that implement them. Over 400 government entities are subject to the SSC.

Building on this effort, with the support of the OECD and financing from the European Union, IGAE is advancing its strategy to improve the SSC. This report presents the IGAE's methodology for the end-to-end process of continuous supervision of public sector entities at the central government level. It also provides examples of good practices from other oversight bodies that have a similar supervisory mandate. The report proposes actions primarily for the IGAE and the ONA to consider in order to improve the effectiveness and impact of the SSC. Proposals for action fall into three related areas: strengthening risk assessments for continuous supervision, enhancing strategies and capacity for data-driven monitoring, and improving transparency, communication and co-ordination.

Chapter 1 introduces the IGAE's continuous supervision mandate, with a focus on the ONA and its responsibilities to deliver the SSC. The chapter provides an overview of "rationality" risk and how the ONA operationalises this concept in its risk assessments and reviews, which focus on 3 entity-level risk factors: 1) compliance with laws and regulations, 2) financial sustainability, and 3) the relevance of the entity in the context of a particular public policy, including whether it duplicates efforts with others. Chapter 1 offers several recommendations for the ONA to strengthen its risk assessments, including the following:

- Formalise the criteria for its automated reviews and clarify how indicators link to the strategy for continuous supervision.
- Leverage the SSC for a broader assessment of sustainability, going beyond current financial indicators.
- Standardise and document processes related to selecting entities for and using the results of control reviews.
- Enhance entity-level assessments of duplication, including consideration of fragmentation and overlap as distinct issues.

Chapter 2 shifts the focus to challenges the ONA faces in terms of its shaping its strategy and building capacity for delivering the SSC in the future. It draws from a broad range of relevant experiences by other audit and control bodies to help shape recommendations to improve the methodology and processes for implementing the SSC. These recommendations focus on various technical aspects, and they include:

- Institutionalise feedback loops to ensure continuous improvement to the SSC and consider further automation as well as the use of dashboards.
- Take additional steps to assess data quality with respect to the SSC.
- Improve the tracking of conclusions and recommendations from continuous supervision activities.
- Invest in the ONA's capacity and specialised data skills for enhancing th SSC.

Chapter 2 also takes into account issues related to transparency, communication and co-ordination. These areas can have an impact on the effectiveness and relevance of the SSC in Spain, as well as the legitimacy of the ONA's efforts as the SSC matures. Drawing inspiration from the Institute of Internal Auditors as well as supreme audit institutions, the chapter offers the following additional recommendation for the ONA:

- Improve the transparency of the SSC, including publishing the annual report and establishing audit committees.
- Enhance co-ordination with key oversight institutions to ensure the effectiveness of the SSC and avoid duplication.
- Develop a communication strategy to demonstrate the value of the SSC to government entities and oversight bodies.

The issues and recommendations presented in the report, while not exhaustive, target many of the ONA's most urgent challenges to delivery its new mandate for continuous supervision. During the course of the project with the OECD, the ONA had already started to take concrete steps to advance the next iteration of the SSC, demonstrating a commitment to ongoing improvement. This commitment is a critical driver for the effectiveness of the SSC to promote accountability and transparency in the Spanish government in the coming years.

1 Refining risk assessments for continuous supervision in Spain

This chapter provides an overview of continuous supervision in Spain, led by the General Comptroller of the State Administration (Intervención General de la Administración del Estado, IGAE) and the National Audit Office (Oficina Nacional de Auditoría, ONA). The chapter describes the objectives and the risk factors that are the focus of the continuous supervision system (sistema de supervisión continua, SSC). It also offers recommendations for the IGAE and the ONA to strengthen its risk assessment processes in relation to the SSC.

Introduction

Various control, inspection and public audit bodies share responsibility for oversight and accountability at the central government level in Spain. This includes the General Comptroller of the State Administration (*Intervención General de la Administración del Estado*, IGAE), which provides three levels of control—review of internal controls, continuous monitoring of financial controls and public internal audit. Within the IGAE, the National Audit Office (*Oficina Nacional de Auditoría*, ONA), plays a critical role as the financial control and internal audit body responsible for the continuous supervision system (*sistema de supervisión continua*, SSC). Other entities with oversight responsibilities include the General Inspection of Services (*Inspección General de Servicios*) within line ministries, which is tasked with reviewing controls related to the effectiveness of an entity's internal processes and procedures (OECD, 2020[1]). In addition, the Court of Audit (*Tribunal de Cuentas*) is responsible for external audits of the economic and financial activity of public entities (Tribunal de Cuentas, n.d.[2]).

As required by the Public Administration Legal Regulation Act of 2015,[1] the IGAE must provide independent oversight when a new public body is created. This involves analysing the rationale for the establishment of the body and assessing possible overlap with existing bodies. In addition, the IGAE must conduct periodic evaluations to determine whether the circumstances justifying the public bodies' existence are still applicable (OECD, 2014[3]).[2] The Act also established the legal framework for the SSC.

This chapter provides an overview of continuous supervision in Spain and the responsibilities of the ONA in relation to the SSC. The ONA first implemented the SSC in 2020, so the processes and methodology are still very much a work in progress. This chapter discusses the ONA's approach as well as the concept or risk in the context of the SSC, including its focus on "rationality risk" and the risk factors established in regulations that that shape the ONA's assessment. The chapter also offers recommendations for how the ONA could strengthen its risk assessment for continuous supervision with emphasis on the following issues:

- formalising criteria for automated reviews and clarifying the linkage between risk indicators and the strategy for continuous supervision
- considering a broader assessment of sustainability, going beyond the focus on financial indicators to the extent its mandate allows
- standardising and documenting selection processes for control reviews and how they are used
- enhancing the approach to continuous supervision by assessing fragmentation and overlap of entities.

The recommendations in the chapter focus on the risk assessment process, and Chapter 2 covers other aspects of the SSC. The chapter highlights the experiences from different countries, such as the United Kingdom, the Netherlands, Brazil and the United States, to support the IGAE in further developing its model for continuous supervision.

Continuous supervision in Spain's public sector

The IGAE's mandate to improve efficiency in the public sector through continuous supervision

The jurisdiction of control for the IGAE's expanded mandate applies to public sector entities linked to or dependent on the General State Administration (*Administración General del Estado*) that are classified as autonomous bodies (*organismos autónomos*) or public business entities (*entidades públicas empresariales*) (Government of Spain, 2015[4]), among others.[3] These entities run the gamut from state-owned corporations to state-run foundations, and vary widely in terms of size, budget, objectives or by line ministries. Table 1.1 shows all public entities subject to continuous supervision.

Table 1.1. Public sector entities in Spain subject to continuous supervision in 2017-19

Legal Form of entity	Characteristics	Number of entities
State trading companies	Public entities owned by the state that engage in commercial activity and operate under commercial law	140
Consortia affiliated to the General State Administration	Provide public services on a partnership basis	71
Autonomous Bodies	Created to deliver public services with more flexibility and are governed similar to line ministries	59
Public sector foundations affiliated with the General State Administration	These entities are designed to use private sector mechanisms	36
Other public bodies affiliated with the General State Administration	Public bodies under the General State Administration that do not come under one of the other categories	31
Unincorporated Funds	Financed by the General State Budget	27
Other public sector entities	Public bodies that do not come under one of the other categories	22
Public business entities	Business entities providing goods and services that are dependent on central ministries	13
State agencies	Tend to have greater management autonomy and often subject to performance-based management contracts with output indicators	9
Independent administrative bodies	First created in the Public Administration Legal Regulation Act of 2015 (*Ley 40/2015 de 1 de octubre de Régimen Jurídico del Sector Público*) and have supervisory functions over a particular sector or economic activity	6
Managing entities and shared service agencies of Social Security	Public bodies affiliated with Social Security	6
Public university	Provider of higher education services	1
Total		**421**

Source: IGAE, Inventory of Public Sector Entities (*Inventario de Entes del Sector Público*, INVESPE).

Continuous supervision activities became the central means for the IGAE to fulfil these responsibilities, which included the design and implementation of the SSC. In Spain, continuous supervision activities are defined as follows:

> *"the set of verifications and analyses, preferably automated, carried out with the purpose of evaluating compliance with the objectives of the continuous supervision system, as well as the specific control actions that, with the same purpose, carried out in the field of permanent financial control or public audit provided for in Law 47/2003, of November 26, General Budgetary." (Government of Spain, 2018[5]).*[4]

The linkage between continuous supervision and the IGAE's existing mandate is therefore explicitly acknowledged and embedded in regulation, which provides specific guidance on co-ordination, planning and execution of these complementary activities. In addition, to further define the role of the IGAE in relation to the SSC, the Ministry of Finance and Civil Service (*Ministerio de Hacienda y Función Pública*) issued a Directive (*Orden HFP/371/2018*) stipulating the methodology for performing continuous supervision (Government of Spain, 2018[5]). Specifically, the IGAE was tasked with the following responsibilities under the Directive:[5]

- Developing continuous supervision activities as required by legislation.
- Planning, performing and evaluating activities in relation to continuous supervision.
- Designing and managing an information system accessible by public sector entities subject to continuous supervision and the corresponding line ministries.
- Issuing instructions specifying the relevant information requirements, criteria and guidelines to ensure the continuous supervision system functions well.

The National Audit Office and its responsibilities for continuous supervision

The IGAE follows a decentralised operating model, with three central service functions to deliver on its core areas of responsibility at the central government level:

- the National Audit Office (*Oficina Nacional de Auditoría*, ONA), the financial control and internal audit body, which is also responsible for the SSC.
- the Public Accounts Office (*Oficina Nacional de Contabilidad*, ONC), responsible for the planning and management of public accounting.
- the Office of Finance and Information Technology (*Oficina de Informática Presupuestaria*, OIP) which designs and implements the IGAE's policies on information technology.

The IGAE also has internal control "delegates" (*intervenciones delegadas*) embedded within line ministries and public sector entities. Delegates act as financial controllers for these government institutions and are responsible for ongoing monitoring of financial controls and public internal audits (IGAE, 2020[6]). Within the IGAE, responsibility for planning, conducting and reporting on the SSC is assigned to the ONA (IGAE, 2020[6]).

While the ONA is the body responsible for co-ordinating and conducting internal audits of public sector entities at central government level, its mandate also includes oversight of control reviews executed by control functions within the IGAE, such as the "delegates" embedded in line ministries or of financial controls over EU funds. It is therefore well-positioned to take a leading role in designing and implementing the SSC. The ONA comprises six divisions to deliver its comprehensive mandate. Currently six members of the ONA staff within the Director's office are leading the planning, design and implementation of the SSC process. This includes the Director, three auditors, a technician and an IT specialist.

Overview of the SSC and defining the concept of rationality risk

Following the addition of continuous supervision to its mandate, the ONA prepared a strategy, approved in 2018 (ONA, 2018[7]), and a methodology (ONA, 2020[8]) for delivering the SSC. The strategy is based on principles of effective internal control (OECD, 2020[9]) and aligns with the objectives for the SSC in the Public Administration Legal Regulation Act. Figure 1.1 illustrates the key elements of the SSC in Spain.

Figure 1.1. Key elements and activities of the ONA's continuous supervision process in Spain

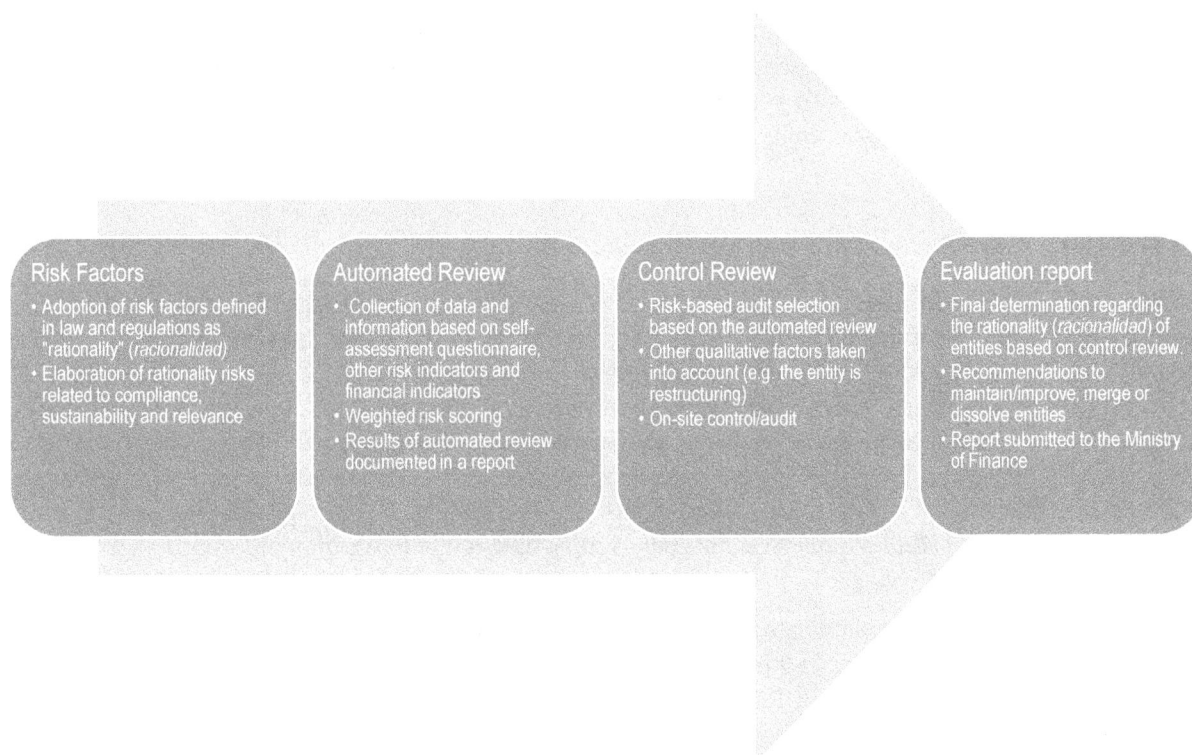

Risk Factors
- Adoption of risk factors defined in law and regulations as "rationality" (*racionalidad*)
- Elaboration of rationality risks related to compliance, sustainability and relevance

Automated Review
- Collection of data and information based on self-assessment questionnaire, other risk indicators and financial indicators
- Weighted risk scoring
- Results of automated review documented in a report

Control Review
- Risk-based audit selection based on the automated review
- Other qualitative factors taken into account (e.g. the entity is restructuring)
- On-site control/audit

Evaluation report
- Final determination regarding the rationality (*racionalidad*) of entities based on control review.
- Recommendations to maintain/improve, merge or dissolve entities
- Report submitted to the Ministry of Finance

Source: OECD authors' elaboration.

Risk factors

Directive HFP/371/2018 provides the basis for how the ONA ultimately defines and interprets risk in the context of the SSC (Government of Spain, 2018[5]). The Directive calls for three levels of verification for the ONA to assess public entities with respect to compliance, financial sustainability and relevance. Taken together, these risk factors form the basis of the concept of "rationality of the structures" (*racionalidad de las estructuras*) of public entities, as defined in the Directive. Through this lens of "rationality," the ONA interprets risk and shapes its automated reviews and continuous supervision methodology. As defined in law, the SSC is not explicitly intended to identify a broader set of strategic, operational or reputational risks, including fraud or corruption risks, if they fall outside the scope of the rationality concept described in Table 1.2.

Table 1.2. Risk factors underpinning rationality risk

Risk Factor	Description
Compliance	The entity complies with laws and regulations
Sustainability	The entity demonstrates financial sustainability.
Relevance	The entity does not duplicate efforts and is the appropriate lead

Source: OECD interpretation of Official Gazette (Boletín Oficial del Estado), (2018[5]).

For public bodies and state-run foundations, financial sustainability includes an assessment of whether to dissolve the entity, taking into consideration its sources of financing, levels of expenditure and investment, as well as the impact, if any, on the General State Budget (*Presupuestos Generales del Estado*). For other categories of public sector entities, financial sustainability is understood, according to the Directive, as the entity's ability to finance current and future expenditure commitments within the limits of applicable rules on public and commercial debt. To establish relevance, the ONA must verify that the reasons for establishing a public sector entity remain, and that the public entity continues to be the most appropriate means for fulfilling the goals entrusted to it. This verification relies, in part, on a review of the entity's strategic action plan. The ONA also verifies whether the entity continues to deliver the services for which it was created, and assesses possible duplication with other entities that could be better placed to deliver the same services.

Automated reviews

"*Automated" reviews* are risk assessments that the ONA conducts based on indicators derived from financial and economic data reported by public sector entities to the IGAE, as well as other qualitative information. The reviews are "automatic" in that data is collected and indicators are generated in an Excel spreadsheet using formulas. Automated reviews apply to all the aforementioned entities that fall under the scope of continuous supervision. The ONA collaborated with the Office of Finance and Information Technology (OIP) within the IGAE on the design of the tool that automatically generates financial and economic indicators and ratios in Excel spreadsheets, drawing data from public financial reporting systems called, *CICEP.red* and *RED.coa*. Entities currently submit data to the IGAE monthly, quarterly or annually in the form of Excel files.

The ONA's methodology for automated reviews produces a risk score based on the following inputs: 1) self-assessment questionnaires; 2) the ONA's consideration of other qualitative risk factors that vary by entity; and 3) financial indicators (OECD, 2020[9]). Figure 1.2 shows the weighting the ONA applies for each input in the total risk score for rationality on a scale from 0 (low) to 3 (high). Specifically, entities with overall scores between 0-1 are considered low risk, between 1-2, at medium risk and 2-3 at higher risk. The score determines which entities warrant a control review. The final output of the automated reviews is called the Automated Actions Report, which communicated the results of the risk analysis.

Figure 1.2. Main data inputs for the automated review and weights for the risk score

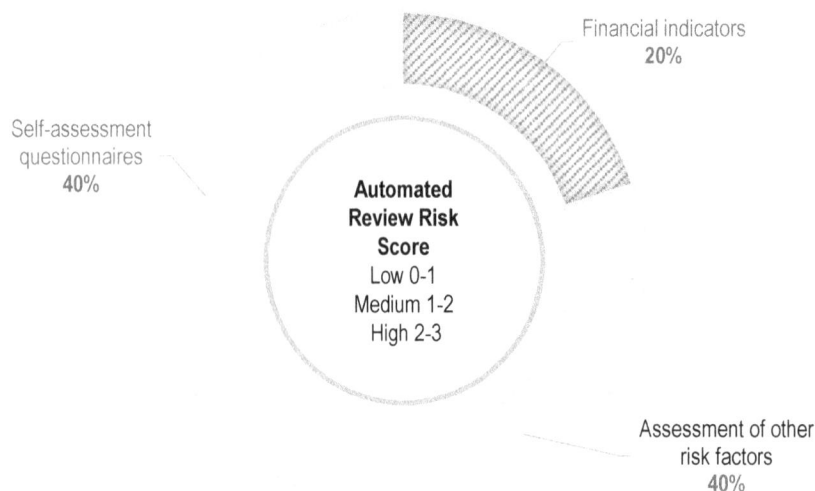

Self-assessment questionnaires
40%

Financial indicators
20%

Automated Review Risk Score
Low 0-1
Medium 1-2
High 2-3

Assessment of other risk factors
40%

Source: the OECD, adapted from (ONA, 2018[7]).

Self-assessment questionnaires

Public sector entities are required to submit self-assessment questionnaires to the ONA as part of the SSC. The questionnaire allows the ONA to collect data on the entity's activities and services delivered, its sources of financing, expenditures and the internal control environment. Entities access and complete the questionnaire using an online form of the *CICEP.red* or *RED.coa* reporting systems, depending on the type of entity. The tool used to generate the indicators and ratios from financial reporting data also aggregates the responses to the self-assessment questionnaires along with any supporting documentation provided by the entity. Analysts performing the SSC risk assessment access the responses and any evidence provided by the entities through Excel files. The leadership of each entity, subject to additional oversight and legal action, certifies the information that the ONA collects as part of the self-assessment. The ONA reviews responses for internal coherence, and if the entity is selected for a control review, it checks whether the information provided in the questionnaire is reliable and accurate.

Other risk factors

"Other qualitative risk factors," a term used in the strategy and methodological documentation for the SSC, makes up 40 percent of the overall risk score for the automated review. These risk factors rely on several sources, including budget data, data from *RED.coa* and information in IGAE's *AUDINet*, which is an application that acts as a central repository for control reports and information about auditing of public accounts. Like the self-assessment questionnaires, these risk factors vary by type of entity. For instance, autonomous bodies and state agencies are subject to the largest number of risk factors, including: how long the agency has been an existence; total expenditure of the entity; the volume of governmental transfers as a percentage of total revenues and income; and the audit opinion of the entity, among other factors. See Table 1.3 for a list of all "other risk factors" for autonomous bodies and state agencies. The ONA gives each of these risk factors a weight, which it uses to calculate an individual risk score. The risk scores are summed for a total valuation of "other qualitative risk factors" for each entity.

Financial indicators

The ONA's financial indicators cover common areas of good practice in public financial management, such as solvency, the entity's ability to meet obligations over the long term, and liquidity, its ability to meet current obligations[6] (IPSASB, 2014[10]). The indicators also consider aspects of operational performance, as well as productivity for entities that have commercial activities. For instance, the indicators for state agencies take into account the ability to cover debt commitments (solvency), but also operational and service delivery components (see Table 1.3).

Table 1.3. Financial indicators used to assess state agencies, among others

These metrics are also applicable to autonomous bodies, consortia, unincorporated funds and other public entities

Solvency	Revenue and Expenditure (%)	Budget management	Liquidity	Activity (Average)
S.1 Debt over assets (%)	CREP.1 Tax revenues/Revenue from ordinary activities	PRE.1 Current budgeted expenditure	L.1 Current ratio	A.1 Units completed/planned units (activities)
S.2 Surplus from ordinary activities	CREP.2 Transfers/Revenue from ordinary activities	PRE.1B Current budgeted expenditure	L.2 Quick ratio	A.4 Population covered (activities)
S.3 Self-financing (%)	CREP.3 VN and PS/Revenue from ordinary activities	PRE.2 Average payment period (days)		A.5 Waiting time for service (days)
S.4 Coverage (%)	CREP.4 Other income/Revenue from ordinary activities	PRE.3 Current budgeted revenue		B.1 Cost of the activity/number of users (days)
S.5 Cash and cash equivalents	CREP.5 Staff costs/Administrative expenses	PRE.3B Current budgeted revenue		B.2 Actual activity cost/projected cost (activities)
	CREP.6 Transfers/Administrative expenses	PRE.4 Average collection period (days)		B.3 Cost of the activity/equivalent units (euros)
	CREP.7 Other expenses/Administrative expenses			C.1 Economic indicators (average)
	CREP.8 Administrative expenses/Revenue from ordinary activities			C.2 Economic indicators (euros)

Source: (ONA, 2020[8]).

The ONA considers additional metrics for entities that undertake commercial activities, such as state trading companies, public business entities and foundations. For example, as these entities can borrow from commercial lenders, bank borrowings as a percentage of liabilities is included as a financial indicator (see Table 1.4).

Table 1.4. Indicators and ratios for public sector entities undertaking commercial activities

Applicable to state trading companies, public business entities and foundations

Financial Management (%)		Structure (%)	Productivity (in EUR 000)
SF.1 Liquidity or acid-test ratio	SF.7 Long-term debt	E.1 Grants/Turnover	P.1 Average staff costs
SF.2 Quick ratio	SF.8 Short-term debt	E.3 Grants/Equity	
SF.3 Solvency	SF.9 Bank borrowings/Liabilities	E.4 Shareholder contributions to equity	
SF.4 Guarantees or Coverage	SF.10 Economic performance	E.5 Related party debt/ Capital	
SF.5 Fixed assets coverage	SF.11 Financial performance	E.6 Grants/Operating profit	
SF.6 Indebtedness			

Source: (ONA, 2020[8]).

Entities are also expected to provide information on annual financing needs (for entities classified as public administrations under the European System of Accounts), gross operating profit, sources of expenditure and investments or sustainability forecasts. Public bodies and state-run foundations are further required to provide annual expenditure and investment reports. Other entities are required to submit sustainability forecasts or at a minimum, a report on their capacity to finance current and long-term commitments within the applicable constraints on public debt.

Control reviews and evaluation reports

The ONA selects public entities for additional scrutiny through on-site "control reviews," which it selects based on the risk scores calculated during the automated review process, as well as consideration of additional qualitative factors. For instance, the ONA will take into account whether the entity has recently gone through a restructuring process, or whether it failed to submit a self-assessment questionnaire. In such cases, entities would be viewed as higher risk and therefore it would be more likely for the ONA to select them for a control review. As part of these reviews, the ONA or delegated entities within the entity may assess whether an entity is achieving its objectives and factor this into its final determination. The reviews culminate with an evaluation report that conveys the ONA's opinion on the rationality of the entity, as defined above, with one of three conclusions:

- *Maintain*—*the* ONA recommends that the entity is maintained in its current form, with possible recommendations for improvement.
- *Merge*—the ONA recommends that the entity merge with another entity with similar objectives and functions.
- *Dissolve*—the ONA determines that the entity is financially unsustainable and should be dissolved.

The ONA reports annually to the Ministry of Finance on the results of individual actions following the control reviews. The Ministry of Finance, in conjunction with the relevant line ministries responsible, table the ONA's recommendations to the Council of Ministers (*Consejo de Ministros*), which ultimately takes the decision (OECD, 2020[9]). This is a key characteristic of the SSC and its target audience. Its effectiveness depends on the judgement and decisions of political leadership who are responsible for the institutional arrangements of government, and have the authority to either accept or reject the ONA's recommendations.

Strengthening risk assessments for continuous supervision

The ONA could formalise the criteria for its automated reviews and clarify how indicators link to the strategy for continuous supervision

Since the ONA first began planning for the SSC in 2018, it has designed the methodology, developed tools to enable the process and completed a full cycle of reviews during a pilot phase in 2019. As the SSC evolves, and prior to its implementation at other levels of government, there are opportunities for the ONA to improve its approach. First, the ONA could formalise the criteria and justifications it has developed for automated reviews, including documenting its rationale for indicators and linkages to the strategy of continuous supervision. In doing so, the ONA would promote transparency of its processes, and improve understanding of how the ONA interprets and acts on risks among entities subject to continuous supervision. The ONA has chosen a comprehensive set of indicators for automated reviews, and it also recognised the need for tailored indicators according to the legal form of the public sector entity. The selection of indicators for financial sustainability in particular reflects a broad consensus on the effectiveness of measuring financial sustainability by evaluating expenditures, revenues, debt and cash management (Pina, Bachiller and Ripoll, 2020[11]). However, not all of the indicators are taken into consideration in the risk weighting for an entity. For instance, Table 1.5 shows the financial indicators for which the ONA collects information on public business entities, including those that contribute to 20% of the automated review risk score and those that are not considered as part of the weighted risk calculation. For purposes of this report, the OECD did not include the weights for each individual indicators, but it is this very information that could be useful for public entities to know.

Table 1.5. Financial indicators for public business entities by risk area

	Structure	Productivity	Financial management
Included in the risk score	• Grants/Turnover • Grants/Equity • Grants/Operating profit	N/A	• Liquidity or acid-test ratio • Quick ratio • Indebtedness • Financial performance
Not included in the risk score	• Shareholder contributions to equity • Related party debt/capital	Average staff costs	• Solvency • Guarantees or Coverage • Fixed assets coverage • Long-term debt • Short-term debt • Bank borrowings/ Liabilities • Economic performance

Note: Although not shown in the table, the weights for public business entities apply to public sector entities classified as "other public entities" (otras entidades de derecho público) with the exception of the average staff costs indicator.
Source: The ONA, Excel file *Indicadores Entes Públicos* (ONA, 2020[12]).

The self-assessment questionnaires follow a similar design. Despite the breadth of the questions in the self-assessment, only some of the responses contribute to an entity's overall risk score for the SSC. For instance, only 11 of the 36 questions for state-run foundations contribute to the overall risk score, as shown in Table 1.6. Other self-assessment questionnaires for different types of entity also draw from a subset of the responses as part of the calculation for 40% of the risk score. The ONA indicated that for the purposes of the pilot, the evaluation team leveraged professional experience and judgement in determining the metrics that would have an assigned risk weighting (OECD, 2020[9]).

Table 1.6. Self-assessment questions for state-run foundations that contribute to the risk score

Question
Are the foundation's objectives included in a strategic action plan that covers justification for its establishment, strategic objectives, description of key activities, timeframe for implementation, budget, system of internal control and performance indicators?
Does the foundation have any objectives or activities that are shared with other foundations or public bodies?
Qualitative value of the patronage received external to the state public sector
Has the Board established an internal control model that aims to provide reasonable assurance of achieving its objectives?
Do you consider that changes have occurred that would justify a review of the foundation's membership or patrons?
Do you believe that there have been changes that justify a review of the aims and objective of the foundation?
In the last five years, has the foundation been subject to actions under Article 132 of the Public Administration Legal Regulation Act of 2015?
Was the strategic action plan of the Foundation approved by the Patron?
In your opinion, have there been changes that could justify the merger of the Foundation with another entity that has similar objectives?
In the last five years, have there been significant changes in the circumstances of the Foundation's patrons?
In your opinion, rate the extent to which the Foundation has the necessary resources (staff, materials, equipment etc.) to effectively achieve its objectives?

Note: Each question receives a different weight determined by the ONA.
Source: Data files provided by the ONA to the OECD with extracts from the CICEP.red and RED.coa (2019).

The ONA's methodology for automated reviews is rigorous and evidence-based, yet it is also complex and underpinned by numerous internal decisions. While the judgement may be sound, the ONA could further clarify why it chooses to include some questions or indicators and not others, as well as provide the rationale to stakeholder for how it determines specific parameters for individual indicators. For instance, ONA officials noted that the questions it does not use for risk score still are important for assessing the internal coherence and reliability of the answers provided. The ONA could also provide additional details in existing methodology documents that explain the criteria for including specific indicators as part of its model, as well as its decisions about assigned weightings.

In addition to formalising the rationale for the metrics used and the corresponding weightings, the ONA could also further clarify the linkage between the rationality risk factors, the selected indicators and its methods for assessing risks via the automated and control reviews. Specifically, this could include explanations as to how the ONA uses information from the self-assessment questionnaires, other risk factors and financial indicators to inform decisions related to the aforementioned risk factors (i.e. compliance, financial sustainability and relevance), as well the selection of entities for further control review. Specifically, in its methodological documentation, the ONA could explain the linkage between the rationality risks and the risk areas identified for each type of entity. For example, in Table 1.4, the ONA could clarify how the indicators related to the risk areas of structure, productivity and financial management directly translate to the 3 areas of rationality risk: compliance, financial sustainability and relevance. This would help to promote transparency, as well as consistency as the SSC matures. It would also would address a need expressed by officials in interviews with the OECD for more information from the ONA about how it uses the information provided for continuous supervision.

For the ONA, the SSC is a new medium for communicating and applying standards in government related to financial management and control. According to ONA officials, the SSC is inspired by the Committee of Sponsoring Entities of the Treadway Commission's (COSO) 2013 Internal Control-Integrated Framework. Box 1.1 presents a self-assessment tool developed by the National Academy for Finance and Economy (NAFE) of the Dutch Ministry of Finance. It supports evaluations and self-assessment, but goes beyond a questionnaire. It offers a self-assessment matrix and clear explanations about financial management and internal control. This has the added benefit of supporting managers in government to learn and apply standards and good practices.

Box 1.1. Netherland's Financial Management and Control Self-Assessment for Government

The National Academy for Finance and Economy (NAFE) of the Dutch Ministry of Finance developed a self-assessment tool to improve public governance, focusing on financial management control (FMC) as a key component of public internal control. The NAFE developed an FMC assessment matrix as a practical tool to support assessments of FMC policies and practices at an institutional level, as well as to aid follow-up evaluations and actions to strengthen FMC. According to the NAFE, reasons for developing such tools include:

- FMC lacks behind the development of internal audit.
- Key elements of FMC are in place, such as financial departments and reporting systems, but operational and implementation challenges remain (including those subsequently listed).
- Excessive operational control by top management.
- Second Line of Defence, i.e., risk management, oversight and monitoring are undeveloped.
- Financial divisions do not support planning and control, except for control of the budget.
- Lack of an entity-wide planning and control mechanism, as well as planning and control at the operational level.
- Blurred lines of responsibility between the second and third lines of defence, i.e., between risk management and the internal audit function.
- Lack of key performance indicators.

The NAFE's FMC assessment matrix allows management to understand the design of their entity assessed against good practice criteria, drawing from the European Union's principles of Public Internal Financial Control (PIFC). Assessors must have excellent knowledge of PIFC, including managerial accountability elements. In addition to managers using the matrix as a self-assessment for their department, internal auditors can make use of the matrix during an entity-wide assessment of currently running FMC systems. Effective implementation of the self-assessment methodology, including completion of the FMC matrix, results in insights about possible actions to improve the FMC configuration and practices. The matrix and results can be shared with management and staff. The table below shows the header row of the matrix followed by an example of how each column can be populated. An actual matrix would include all key components of the internal control system, such as the internal audit function, as well as many other key variables and assessment impacts.

Table 1.7. Illustrative example of select components of an FMC assessment matrix

Key component of internal control	Key variables	Assessment aspects	Indicators	Sources	Methodological approach
FMC within the primary processes/ programmes /projects (I)	Configuration of Managerial Accountability (composition of the accountability triangle: Responsibility, Accountability and Authority) (I.1)	Responsibility: there is a delegated mandate structure (tasks/obligations) described which is aligned with the entityal structure	FMC within the primary processes/programmes /projects (I)	Configuration of Managerial Accountability (composition of the accountability triangle: Responsibility, Accountability and Authority) (I.1)	Responsibility: there is a delegated mandate structure (tasks/obligations) described which is aligned with the entityal structure.

	Alignment of the managerial accountability configuration (I.2)	Responsibilities are well aligned and in balance with accountability obligations and granted authorities (I.2.1)	Alignment of the three elements of the accountability triangle	Internal regulations/process /programme descriptions	Study relevant internal regulations and assess to what extent the responsibilities, accountability and authorities are balanced with each other
FMC through supportive oversight/ controlling /monitoring processes (II)	Managerial Accountability (II.1)	Responsibility: The division of tasks and responsibilities between supportive second-line functions and first-line departments is clear and unambiguous. (II.1.1)	It is clear how division of tasks and responsibilities between first-line primary processes and second-line supportive functions are divided	• Internal regulations/ procedures • Operational Management •Management of supportive functions (e.g. financial department, planning department, HR, IT)	Check the internal regulations/procedures and see if a clear division of tasks between first and second line can be distinguished. Is it described at all? In interviews: try to determine if the division of tasks matches the philosophy of first and second line or not. If the distinction between first and second line is blurry: describe it

Source: (The Dutch Ministry of Finance, March 2018[13]).

Finally, the FMC assessment matrix relies on the Institute of Internal Auditors' Three Lines Model. In particular, according to this model, operational managers are the first line. They are responsible for implementing and maintaining effective internal control while assessing risks to operations and strategic objectives. The various oversight, risk management and compliance functions overseeing the operational management make up the second line. These functions are responsible for support, monitoring, oversight and control over the first line. The internal audit function is the third line, and it provides independent assurance on the functioning of the first two lines. Each of these three "lines" are reflected in the FMC assessment matrix, since they play distinct roles within the entity's wider governance framework.

Source: The Dutch Ministry of Finance (March 2018[13]), *Good Financial Governance and Public Internal Control, Presentation to the OECD.*

Officials of public entities, interviewed by the OECD, were broadly supportive of the ONA and the recommendations it has made to date through the SSC process. In one interview, an entity raised the issues of the administrative burden the SSC creates, particularly concerning the need to compile and respond to the questionnaires. To avoid duplication of effort and limit the administrative burden on entities, only information not readily accessible by the IGAE and the ONA is required of entities as part of the SSC process (Government of Spain, 2018[5]). Moreover, to promote efficiency, the technical requirements are the same for both financial reporting and the SSC. The self-assessment questionnaires themselves, conducted on an annual basis, consist of approximately 35 questions. These measures suggest that the ONA has taken into account the burden it places on public entities in the design of the SSC. Nonetheless, the process of formalising its criteria and further documenting its rationale for its methodology could lead to in even leaner and less burdensome set of self-assessment questionnaires, which currently do not use all the questions for risk scoring as it is.

The SSC makes effective use of financial indicators, but opportunities remain to leverage the process for a broader assessment of sustainability

As discussed, one of the three risk factors that the ONA focuses on when assessing rationality risk is financial sustainability (the others being compliance and relevance). The assessment of financial indicators and ratios is a useful starting point for the ONA to evaluate financial sustainability of public sector entities in line with the Directive on continuous supervision. However, in other OECD countries, many audit bodies are incorporating a focus on y financial or economic metrics and increasingly considering the value of environmental and social benefits that the entity provides. One way the ONA can advance its efforts to enhance the impact and effectiveness of the SSC is to consider broader notions of long-term financial sustainability as part of its risk assessment process. To do this, the ONA would require an amendment to the Public Administration Legal Regulation Act of 2015 (*Ley 40/2015 de 1 de octubre de Régimen Jurídico del Sector Público*). The amendment would help the ONA to further modernise the SSC for future iterations, and support a longer-term vision for government and society that transcends the narrow interpretation of sustainability to short-term financial concerns.

Definitions of financial sustainability in the public sector context can vary. One common factor in most definitions is the likelihood of the failure of public bodies with significant liabilities or debt burdens (Pina, Bachiller and Ripoll, 2020[11]). However, financial sustainability of public entities is more complex than this one factor. The International Public Sector Accounting Standards Board (IPSASB) defines long-term fiscal or financial sustainability as a circumstance in which a public sector entity is able to achieve its goals for service delivery and meet its financial commitments both now and in the future (IPSASB, 2013[14]). This definition is similar to that of financial sustainability in the Directive on the SSC but with an added emphasis on service delivery.

In the IPSASB's recommended guidance for public sector entities, consideration of financial sustainability is broader than accounting information from financial statements. It includes projected cash inflows and outflows related to the provision of goods, services and programmes providing public services using current policy assumptions over a specified period. The IPSASB identified three inter-related dimensions of long-term financial sustainability—service, revenue and debt—as well as two aspects that affect each dimension: *capacity*, the entity's ability to change or influence the dimension, and *vulnerability*, the extent of the entity's dependence on factors outside its control or influence:

- **Service**: the projected volume and quantity of public services and entitlements to beneficiaries that an entity can deliver. This view of financial sustainability takes into account policy assumptions related to revenue from taxation or other sources, as well as debt constraints, and considers the impact on the entity's ability to deliver services.

- **Revenue**: impact of taxation levels and other sources of revenue on the provision of services while staying within debt constraints. In this dimension, the entity considers its capacity to vary tax receipt levels, modify or add sources of revenue. It also considers the entity's vulnerabilities to outside sources of revenue. For example, if an entity's inter-governmental transfers are legally mandated, its revenue streams are likely to be more stable.

- **Debt**: considers debt levels and projected debt levels over the length of the assessment period in light of expected service provision commitments. In this dimension, an entity considers its capacity to meet its financial commitments on time or to refinance or incur additional debt where necessary. The level of net debt, or the amount spent providing goods and services in the past that need to be funded in the future is a key indicator as illustrated in Figure 1.3.

Figure 1.3. Relationships between the dimensions of long-term financial sustainability

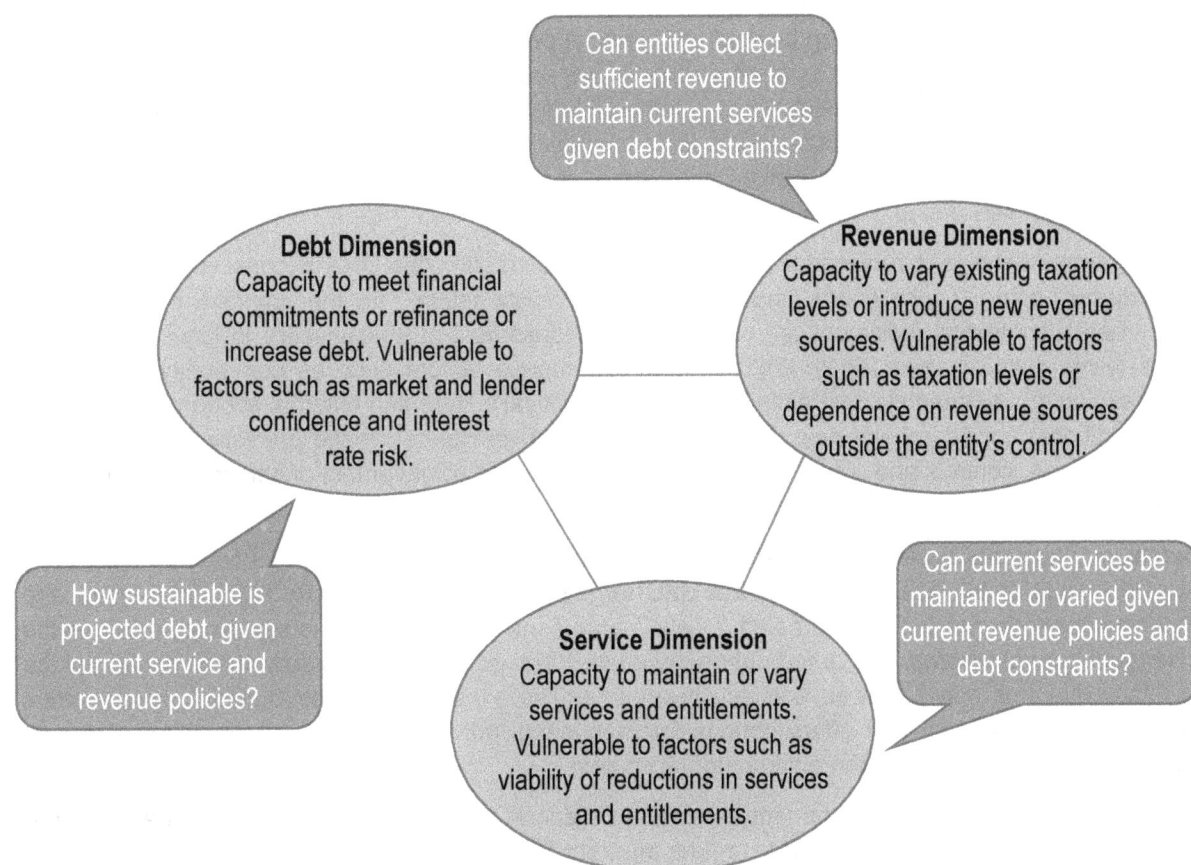

Note: The original title is "Relationships between the dimensions of long-term *fiscal* sustainability."
Source: (IPSASB, 2013[14]).

Assessments of financial sustainability can use a broad range of data such as financial and non-financial information about future economic and demographic conditions, assumptions about country and global trends such as productivity, relative competitiveness of the economy (at national, state or local levels) and demographic variables (IPSASB, 2013[14]). The ONA already considers several factors related to revenue and debt dimensions and considers performance aspects of the entities it monitors as part of the SSC. Building on this, provided it obtains the legal mandate, the ONA could enhance its focus on the service dimension in the IPSASB model. For example, the ONA could incorporate questions and qualitative indicators into its self-assessment questionnaires and "other risk factors" that provide insights about the service dimension of, such as:

- Does the entity(s) have the capacity to vary volume or quantity of services it provides?
- Is the entity(s) vulnerable to factors such as an inability to vary service levels or the unwillingness of recipients to accept reduced services?
- Are expenditures on specific programmes expected to increase at a higher rate than the general level of expenditure?
- Do entity(s) with capital-intensive activities account for the expected useful lives or replacement values of property, plant and equipment?

Such questions are useful for assessing medium- to long-term financial sustainability because they allow for comparison between an entity's current or projected commitments to a future state, based on reasonable assumptions. The ONA could also add performance-related indicators that are relevant for not only the objectives of individual entities, but also for transversal policies that rely on the effectiveness and efficiency of multiple entities or programmes. This could include indicators related to health, education and welfare policies. For instance, going beyond the financial performance of an entity, the ONA's indicators could reflect the cost of healthcare as a percentage of projected revenue from taxes and other sources, or as a percentage of changes in the estimated volume of beneficiaries. This analysis would provide insights about potential systemic challenges related to the sustainability health provision. Such analysis would also provide the entities responsible, as well as consumers of the ONA's reports, with deeper insights about the functioning of services and use of taxpayer money.

As a long-term objective, a renewed legal mandate would also allow the ONA to consider environmental (i.e. external context) challenges that could affect sustainability in the context of the SSC. Environmental/contextual indicators are crucial in the assessment of sustainability in local government entities (Pina, Bachiller and Ripoll, 2020[11]) and encompass factors such as community needs and resources, intergovernmental constraints, disaster risk, political culture and external economic conditions. These additional considerations help decision-makers to govern better, make predictive decisions and enhance policies, controls and resource investment to ensure the achievement of objectives in relation to the rationality risks of compliance, sustainability and relevance.

In addition, taking into account the broader context could also have practical implications for the ONA's unit of analysis for the SSC. Currently, the SSC targets individual entities, according to the law and regulations that governs it. The automated reviews capture information related to specific entities and the subsequent control reviews are carried out on the entities that pose the highest risk. In the context of the SSC, the ONA has only reviewed entities one-by-one. The experience of the United Kingdom offers insights into an approach that offers options for monitoring individual institutions and across several institutions, taking into account the environmental context.

In the United Kingdom., the government established triennial reviews to ensure that non-departmental public bodies (NDPBs) were subjected to regular and robust monitoring.[7] The purpose is similar to that of the ONA's SSC, albeit with a greater focus on outcomes and impact. The reviews act as mechanisms to ensure the NDPBs exist for a clear purpose, deliver the services users want, maximise the value for money for the taxpayer and confirm they have not outlived their useful purpose (UK Cabinet Office, 2015[15]). Since the launch of the programme in 2011, departments have reviewed hundreds of entities and recommended the dissolution of NDPBs. The success of the triennial review programme informed the design of the transformation methodology for the 2015 to 2020 Public Bodies Transformation Programme (see Box 1.2).

Box 1.2. The 2016-20 Public Bodies Transformation Programme of the United Kingdom

In April 2011, the UK Cabinet Office announced a triennial review starting in 2011 for all non-departmental public bodies (NDPBs) still in existence following the reforms brought about by the Public Bodies Act. According to the Cabinet Office, the review led to "fewer, more accountable and more efficient" government; the triennial reviews brought together public bodies across departments to deliver greater transformation than departments could deliver alone. Building on this effort, the Cabinet Office established the 2016-20 Public Bodies Transformation Programme. The Department-led reviews conducted as part of this programme provide regular assurance concerning the continuing need, efficiency and good governance of public bodies. The programme is two-pronged, consisting of "tailored reviews" and "functional reviews."

Tailored Reviews

Tailored reviews extend the scope of the triennial review process to include executive agencies and non-ministerial departments. Each body is subject to a tailored review. The scope of the tailored review can be carried out in the context of departmental or functional reviews, described below. Their purposes it to challenge and provide assurance on the continuing need for an individual public entity in terms of both function and form. Reviews focus on the entity's capacity for delivering more effectively and efficiently, including identifying the potential for efficiency savings, and where appropriate, its ability to contribute to economic growth. The Cabinet Office's guidance indicates that the review "should include an assessment of the performance of the entity or assurance that processes are in place for making such assessments." Reviews also take into account control and governance arrangements in place to ensure compliance with principles of good corporate governance.

Functional Reviews

Functional reviews look across departments and examine holistically the functions of several public bodies in similar or related areas of government. This approach will identify opportunities for reform that cannot be revealed by reviewing bodies one by one. The first review covers bodies with regulatory functions. This and subsequent reviews will be delivered through partnership with public bodies, and departments.

The Cabinet Office oversees the reviews. The guidance for the reviews establishes a principle of openness, and encourage public entities to publish results of reviews. In addition to transparency, other key principles for conducting the reviews include proportionality, challenge, being strategic, pace and inclusivity. The report of the reviews include recommendations to improve the effectiveness and efficiency for government, including evidence to substantiate judgements and consideration of the value for money for taxpayers.

Source: (UK Cabinet Office, 2019[16]) and (UK Cabinet Office, 2015[15]).

As described in Box 1.2, the UK's programme has a similar objective to the SSC as a way to provide continuous assurance that public entities remain relevant, needed and efficient in their operations. The UK's guidance for tailored reviews provides some insights as to how the ONA could enhance future iterations of the SSC. The guidance calls for reviews that are challenging and take a "first principles" approach to whether each function is 1) still needed; 2) still being delivered; 3) carried out effectively; and 4) contributes to the core business of the entity, the sponsor department and to the government as a whole (UK Cabinet Office, 2019[16]). The environment (the external context discussed previously), as well as broader governance and financial issues like savings in relation to digital transformation, also are important considerations for the tailored reviews. For instance, the guidance highlights the following questions for assessing both efficiency and costs of digital transformation, as well as the impact on users of services:

- What is the current spend in this area or areas?
- How many transactions are received by the service per channel (online, phone, paper, face to face)
- How many of these transactions end in an outcome, and a user's intended outcome?
- How many phone calls, letters or in-person visits are there to the service?
- What are the reasons for those phone calls, letters or in-person visits (e.g. to get information, chase progress, challenge a decision)?
- What will the expenditure be after transformation?
- When will savings start to be realised?
- What will be the reduction in average cost per transaction, service or channel?
- Is there potential in other areas of the public body's activities to consider digital work that will contribute to spending reductions and improved services? (UK Cabinet Office, 2019[16])

In addition to being more performance-oriented, another key difference, which could help the ONA develop the SSC further, is the UK's model of finding opportunities for improvement that are not identifiable by assessing public bodies individually or one-by-one. The UK's functional reviews are by definition cross-departmental, and therefore they provide a more comprehensive picture than the tailored reviews concerning issues that affect or implicate multiple entities. The ONA's SSC provides a foundation for expanding the current self-assessment questionnaires, or alternatively the lines of inquiry as part of control reviews, in the same way. In addition, the SSC covers entities that are the equivalent to NDPBs in the UK, so many of the questions are directly relevant for the ONA's approach.

The ONA could standardise and document its process for selecting entities for control reviews, as well as the process and use of the reviews themselves

As noted, the ONA uses automated reviews to identify entities that pose a higher risk in terms of the concept of a rationality, in particular, the risk of the entity being non-compliant with laws, financially unsustainable, or irrelevant and duplicative relative to other entities. Based on this assessment and the resulting risk score, the ONA selects entities for further control reviews. During the pilot phase of the SSC, the ONA completed automated reviews of 421 entities. It selected nine entities for the control review. In interviews, the ONA explained this selection process, described below. However, the ONA could standardise and document its approach and criteria for decision-making to improve future supervision activities and promote greater transparency of the SSC.

In the SSC strategy, the ONA anticipated defining criteria to streamline and possibly automate the decision-making process for selecting entities to review. However, the ONA has yet to do this in its current methodology. The ONA indicated during interviews that the pilot phase of the SSC served to develop a baseline both for the metrics used for the automated review and for the criteria used in selecting entities for control review by an evaluation team. The evaluation team reviewed the risk score from the automated review with ONA analysts, and applied selection criteria to determine which entities warranted further review. The ONA indicated that the selection criteria included consideration of recommendations from other control reviews or public audits.

The ONA noted that consistency in the application of the selection criteria was achieved through discussion and agreement with the evaluation team for the nine entities reviewed during the pilot. As the SSC evolves from a pilot to full implementation, the ONA could benefit from formalising this process, including the selection criteria, in its methodology documents for the SSC. This will help future evaluations teams to carry out the SSC, and promote consistency and standardisation in the selection process. As the SSC matures, the ONA could periodically review and update this guidance and criteria for relevance and adjust as necessary. Box 1.3 provides some insights as to how the Federal Court of Accounts in Brazil (*Tribunal de Contas da União*, TCU) guides auditors in selecting entities for control actions.

Box 1.3. Assessing risks for audit selection by the Brazilian Federal Court of Accounts

To further align its practices with the International Standards of the Supreme Audit Institutions (ISSAI), the Federal Court of Accounts in Brazil (*Tribunal de Contas da União*, TCU) develop a process for its audit teams to systematically assess risks and key challenges in order to select audit subjects. To support this initiative, TCU developed guidance for its teams that explains the methodology and steps that auditors can take to conduct the risk assessments. The methodology encourages broad participation of internal stakeholders, including directors and auditors, as well external experts.

The guidance provides auditors with insights for assessing risk factors, materiality, relevance and opportunities concerning audit subjects. The "relevance" element considers whether audit subject or the implicates pressing issues of interest to society that are under public debate. The guidance outline how assessments are conducted, and it describes TCU's severity index, represented as follows:

*Severity Index = (Social Impact + Economic Impact) * Probability * Trend*

TCU scores "social impact" and "economic impact" variables on a scale from 1 (low) to 5 (high). "Probability" and "trend" are variables that are both represented by percentages. Multiplying by the perceived trend allows TCU to decrease o increase the severity of a problem based on the auditors' perceived direction of the problem (i.e. trending better or worse). TCU recognises the need for individual audit teams to tailor the guidance and it clearly articulate measures of quality for auditors. The methodology is designed to be flexible so that it is useful to different types of audit teams, as well as to account for different data requirements, availability and resources. To ensure the quality of the selection process, the guidance encourages audit teams to do the following:

- obtain comprehensive and quality data on the universe of control under its jurisdiction
- invite experts to assist in the analysis of related topics
- seek internal guidance and support throughout the process
- make appropriate use of the internal tools (i.e. a selection support system)
- seek to involve the entire team of auditors in the discussion and analysis process
- schedule sufficient resources and time to carry out the activities
- properly document all stages of the process, so that the basis for the decisions adopted is demonstrated and that the information collected is preserved, enabling its eventual use in inspection processes or for planning work in future years.

TCU considers the relevance criteria when assessing the economic and social impact. Determining the scoring for individual variables relies on the professional judgement and expertise of auditors, as well as data and information collected during the selection process. The TCU promotes other forms of analysis to contemplate its risk assessments, such as Ishikawa Analysis and Problem Trees. Heads of audit units must approved the determinations and scoring related to risks. Once the TCU completes its analysis, it selects subjects for control. The guidance maps out each of these phases so that auditors have a step-by-step understanding of the entire process.

Source: (Federal Court of Accounts of Brazil, 2016[17]).

In addition, the control review follows a methodology specifically designed for the SSC (*actuaciones de control individualizadas*) which indicates the steps that an evaluator should follow. However, the methodology does not articulate the strategic elements for consideration or criteria underpinning the decision making for the opinion. As with the selection criteria for entities warranting further control review, the ONA indicated that the recommendations and opinions for the evaluation reports produced in the pilot were achieved through discussion and agreement with the evaluation team on a case-by-case basis.

The ONA could benefit from further defining the principles, guidance and criteria that evaluators and auditors can consider when forming recommendations and decisions about the rationality of entity. It could also clarify the process downstream, after the completion of the control review and the communication of the results in an evaluation report to the Ministry of Finance. For instance, the Directive (*Orden HFP/371/2018*) requires the ONA to include the response of an entity's governing body or line ministry in its opinion; however, it does not provide guidance on actions to be taken in the event that there is a difference in opinion between the ONA and the line ministry.

ONA officials informed the OECD that the public entity evaluates the results of the SSC, and if it disagrees with IGAE's conclusions, it would be elevated to the Ministry of Finance to advance the decision and possibly negotiate with the entity. Clarifying this process and decision-making criteria, in co-ordination with policymakers, could have several effects. First, it would help to promote more transparency of the SSC and important decisions about how the government is structured and taxpayer money is used. Second, it would be useful for subjects of the SSC to understand more clearly the rationale for conclusions and recommendations proposed. Lastly, clarifying how the results of controls reviews and the evaluation reports are and should be used—as well as further documenting the expectations, roles and responsibilities in this regard—would help to promote political accountability of the SSC. In particular, enhanced transparency and clarification of the process would help to promote ownership and responsibility among the Council of Ministers for decisions taken, or not taken, as a result of the ONA's continuous supervision activities.

The ONA could enhance its approach to assessing duplication, including consideration of fragmentation and overlap

A key component of the CORA reforms was to reduce duplication and overlap within the general state administration as well as between the state administration and the autonomous or local governments. This is reflected in the SSC as a key risk factor, described as "relevance" for purposes of this report (see Figure 1.3 above). The CORA sub-commission defined "overlap" as different public entities providing identical services to identical recipients or public entities with similar missions acting on the same subjects. In conjunction with the Sub-Commission on Institutional Administration, the Sub-Commission on Overlap aimed to improve efficiency by streamlining the number of public sector institutions, companies and foundations.

To assess duplication, the ONA compares the powers assigned to the entity subject to the SSC with those of other entities that have similar objectives. The ONA verifies that the entities operate in the same or similar environment and scope. The ONA typically carries out the analysis manually, consisting of a review of relevant norms, statutes and other documentation for establishing the entities. Budget information, activity codes and other information or data can also be inputs for the ONA to determine whether duplication exists.

To enhance this approach, the ONA can draw lessons and inspiration from the work of supreme audit institutions (SAIs).In the United States, the Government Accountability Office (GAO) developed a unique approach to assessing not only duplication, but also fragmentation and overlap (see Box 1.2 for further explanation). GAO's work promotes policy coherence in government, and it recognises that duplication or overlap is not always negative. For instance, complex policy issues involving multiple actors can benefit from multi-stakeholder insights and contributions, particularly in the case of transversal policies that cut across sectors and involve different entities. In 2015, the GAO issued a manual for assessing duplication, fragmentation and overlap. Notably for the ONA as it consider formalising its process, the manual includes guidance for auditors as well as policymakers and managers in government. It highlights four key steps:

1. Identify fragmentation, overlap, and duplication among a selected set of programmes and understand how the selected programmes are related.
2. Identify the potential positive and negative effects of any fragmentation, overlap, or duplication found in Step 1.
3. Validate the effects identified in Step 2 and assess and compare the fragmented, overlapping, or duplicative programmes in order to determine their relative performance and cost-effectiveness.
4. Identify options to reduce or better manage the negative effects of fragmentation, overlap, and duplication (US Government Accountability Office, 2015[18]).

The ONA could consider explicitly incorporating fragmentation and overlap into its analysis. At a minimum, this could include adding additional questions to the self-assessment process or in an internal guide for auditors to conduct control reviews that would them to identify duplication, fragmentation and overlap. The ONA considers some of these key questions already, although it could do so more formally and systematically:

- How are entities or programmes related to each other?
- Which entities or programmes are unnecessarily duplicating others?
- Where can efficiencies be found between programmes with shared goals?
- What relations do these programmes have with others?
- Are there legitimate reasons for competition among or redundancies between entities or programmes?

A more robust assessment of duplication, fragmentation and overlap would likely require more resources than the ONA currently has for the SSC. However, the benefit from a government-wide perspective in the US context is considerable. As noted in Box 1.4, the GAO identified approximately USD 429 billion in total financial benefits as a result of actions taken to address GAO's recommendations related to fragmentation, duplication and overlap.

Box 1.4. The US Government Accountability Office's assessments of fragmentation, duplication and overlap

The Government Accountability Office (GAO) is required by law to conduct routine investigations to identify federal programmes, agencies, offices, and initiatives with duplicative goals and activities within departments and government-wide. GAO also must report annually to Congress on its findings, including the costs of fragmentation, overlap and duplication in government, as well as recommendations for Congress to address it. The figure below shows how GAO defines these concepts.

Figure 1.4. Definitions of Fragmentation, Overlap and Duplication

Fragmentation refers to those circumstances in which more than one federal agency (or more than one organisation within an agency) is involved in the same broad area of national need and opportunities exist to improve service delivery.

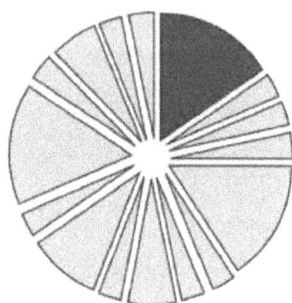

Overlap occurs when multiple agencies or programmes have similar goals, engage in similar activities or strategies to achieve them or target similar beneficiaries.

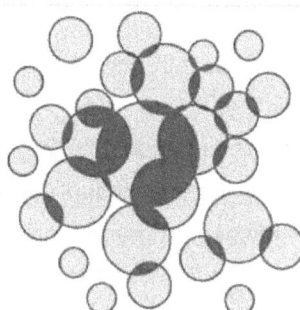

Duplication occurs when two or more agencies or programmes are engaged in the same activities or provide the same services to the same beneficiaries.

The GAO collects and analyses data on costs and potential savings to the extent they are available. GAO uses the information to identify potential financial and other benefits that can result from addressing fragmentation, overlap, or duplication, or taking advantage of other opportunities for cost savings and enhancing revenues.

Ensuring the reliability of data

GAO assesses the reliability of any computer-processed data that materially affects findings, including cost savings and revenue enhancement estimates. GAO reports on data reliability for each source and area it assesses. The steps taken to assess the reliability of data vary, but generally aim at fulfilling auditing requirements that data be sufficiently reliable and fit-for-purpose. The steps GAO takes to assess data reliability for this work can include:

- Reviewing published documentation about the data system, including reviews of the data by the inspector general or others.
- Interviews with the entities' or external officials to better understand system controls and process for producing the data, as well as any limitations associated with the data.
- Electronic testing of the data to see whether values in the data conform to what is said in interviews or documentation regarding valid values.
- Comparison of data to source documents, as well as other sources for corroboration.

Results of 2020 activities

GAO's 2020 report identifies 29 new areas where a broad range of government entities may be able to enhance efficiency or effectiveness. For each area, GAO suggests actions that Congress or executive branch agencies could take to reduce, eliminate, or better manage fragmentation, overlap, or duplication, or achieve other financial benefits. GAO also monitors actions taken to address its previous recommendations. GAO identified approximately USD 429 billion in total financial benefits as a result of steps either the Congress or government entities have taken to address GAO's recommendations related to fragmentation, duplication and overlap.

Source: (US Government Accountability Office, 2020[19]).

Conclusion

This chapter describes Spain's approach to continuous supervision and how the IGAE and the ONA have scoped the assessment of risks around the concept of "rationality risk." Spain's regulations provide the basis for how the ONA ultimately defines and interprets risk in the context of the SSC (Government of Spain, 2018[5]), calling for three levels of verification for the ONA to assess public entities with respect to compliance, financial sustainability and relevance. The ONA has developed a solid risk assessment methodology, which it first implemented in 2020. Building on this early model, the chapter offers recommendations for the ONA to continue advancing its risk assessment processes and methodology for continuous supervision.

The recommendations reflect opportunities for the ONA to formalise the criteria for its automated reviews and clarify how its risk indicators link to the strategy for continuous supervision. In addition, while the ONA makes effective use of financial indicators as part of the SSC, it could further leverage the process for a broader assessment of sustainability, including greater consideration for long-term financial sustainability and performance-related indicators. The ONA could also emphasise standardisation as it moves ahead with the next iterations of the SSC. This could involve documenting processes for selecting entities for control reviews and clarifying the process and use of the reviews themselves. Finally, the ONA could enhance its current approach for assessing duplication of government entities and programmes by incorporating analyses that also consider fragmentation and overlap. These are related but distinct challenges, and the SSC could be an effective tool for understanding and monitoring these issues in government.

References

Federal Court of Accounts of Brazil (2016), *Guidelines for Selecting Objects and Control Actions*, https://portal.tcu.gov.br/fiscalizacao-e-controle/auditoria/selecao-de-objetos-e-acoes-de-controle/. [17]

Government of Spain (2018), *Official Gazette (Boletín Oficial del Estado)*, https://www.boe.es/eli/es/o/2018/04/09/hfp371. [5]

Government of Spain (2015), *Official Gazette (Boletín Oficial del Estado)*, https://www.boe.es/buscar/act.php?id=BOE-A-2015-10566. [4]

IGAE (2020), *Memoria de actividades 2019*. [6]

IPSASB (2014), *The Conceptual Framework for General Purpose Financial Reporting by Public Sector Entities*, International Public Sector Accounting Standards Board, https://www.ipsasb.org/publications/conceptual-framework-general-purpose-financial-reporting-public-sector-entities-3. [10]

IPSASB (2013), *Recommended Practice Guideline: Reporting on the Long-Term Sustainability of an Entity's Finances*, International Public Sector Accounting Standards Board, https://www.ipsasb.org/publications/recommended-practice-guideline-1. [14]

OECD (2020), *OECD Fact-Finding Interview with the Inspector General of Services for the Ministry of Finance (Inspección General de Servicios del Ministerio de la Hacienda)*. [1]

OECD (2020), *OECD Fact-finding interviews with the National Audit Office (Oficina Nacional de Auditoría, ONA)*. [9]

OECD (2014), *Spain: From Administrative Reform to Continuous Improvement*, OECD Public Governance Reviews, OECD Publishing, Paris, https://dx.doi.org/10.1787/9789264210592-en. [3]

ONA (2020), *Indicadores Entes Públicos*. [12]

ONA (2020), *Metodología relativa a las actuaciones de supervisión continua automatizadas*. [8]

ONA (2018), *Estrategia del Sistema de Supervisión Continua (2018-2020)*. [7]

Pina, V., P. Bachiller and L. Ripoll (2020), "Testing the Reliability of Financial Sustainability. The Case of Spanish Local Governments", *Sustainability*, Vol. 12, http://dx.doi.org/10.3390/su12176880. [11]

The Dutch Ministry of Finance (March 2018), *Good Financial Governance and Public Internal Control, Presentation to the OECD*. [13]

Tribunal de Cuentas (n.d.), *Función de Fiscalización*, https://www.tcu.es/tribunal-de-cuentas/es/fiscalizacion/funcion-de-fiscalizacion/ (accessed on November 2020). [2]

UK Cabinet Office (2019), *Tailored Reviews: Guidance on Reviews of Public Bodies*, https://assets.publishing.service.gov.uk/government/uploads/system/uploads/attachment_data/file/802961/Tailored_Review_Guidance_on_public_bodies_-May-2019.pdf. [16]

UK Cabinet Office (2015), *Public Bodies 2015*,
https://assets.publishing.service.gov.uk/government/uploads/system/uploads/attachment_dat
a/file/506880/Public_Bodies_2015_Web_9_Mar_2016.pdf.

[15]

UK Cabinet Office (2014), *Triennial Reviews: Guidance on Reviews of Non-Departmental Public Bodies*,
https://assets.publishing.service.gov.uk/government/uploads/system/uploads/attachment_dat
a/file/332147/Triennial_Reviews_Guidance.pdf.

[20]

US Government Accountability Office (2020), *2020 Annual Report: Additional Opportunities to Reduce Fragmentation, Overlap, and Duplication and Achieve Billions in Financial Benefits, GAO-20-440SP*, https://www.gao.gov/assets/710/707031.pdf.

[19]

US Government Accountability Office (2015), *Fragmentation, Overlap, and Duplication: An Evaluation and Management Guide*, https://www.gao.gov/assets/gao-15-49sp.pdf.

[18]

Notes

[1] Part II, Chapter II, Organisation and Functioning of the state institutional public sector. Article 81.2 requires public administrations to establish a system of continuous supervision of their dependent entities, justifying the reasons for their existence and financial sustainability and include proposals to maintain, transform or dissolve the entity. Article 84 defines the categories of public sector entities in scope for continuous supervision and efficiency control reviews while Article 85 defines the roles and responsibilities of the *Hacienda*, the IGAE and the ministerial inspection units.

[2] Chapter 2 Administrative Rationalisation and Multi-Level Governance.

[3] Article 84.

[4] Article 10 Continuous Supervision Activities *Actuaciones de supervisión continua Orden HFP/371/2018*.

[5] Article 6 Role of the IGAE *Funciones de la Intervención General del Estado Orden HFP/371/2018*.

[6] Definitions of solvency and liquidity are based on the Conceptual Framework for General Purpose Financial Reporting by Public Sector Entities issued by the International Public Sector Accounting Standards Board (IPSASB) (IPSASB, 2014[10]).

[7] Non-Departmental Public Bodies (NDPB) is an administrative term for those public bodies that operate at arm's length from Ministers, but for which Ministers are ultimately accountable. NDPBs can be statutory or non-statutory (UK Cabinet Office, 2014[20]).

2 Strategies for data-driven and transparent continuous supervision in Spain

This chapter discusses strategic and operational issues for the General Comptroller of the State Administration (Intervención General de la Administración del Estado, IGAE) and the National Audit Office (Oficina Nacional de Auditoría, ONA) to further improve the continuous supervision system (Sistema de Supervisión Continua, SSC). It offers recommendations for the IGAE and the ONA to enhance the strategy and capacity for data-driven monitoring, as well as to improve the transparency, communication and co-ordination concerning the SSC.

Introduction

The current form of continuous supervision in Spain has its roots in the 2013 reform package of the Commission for the Reform of the Public Administration (CORA), which proposed regular monitoring and evaluation of the "rationality" of public sector entities in Spain (OECD, 2014[1]). This concept was soon codified in the Public Administration Legal Regulation Act of 2015 (*Ley 40/2015 de 1 de octubre de Régimen Jurídico del Sector Público*)[1] and outlined further in a 2018 Directive (*Orden HFP/371/2018*) that stipulated the methodology for performing continuous supervision. While the legal and regulatory framework developed over this span of five years, the General Comptroller of the State Administration (*Intervención General de la Administración del Estado*, IGAE), and more specifically, the National Audit Office (*Oficina Nacional de Auditoría*, ONA) have had comparatively less time to implement the continuous supervision system (*sistema de supervisión continua*, SSC).

At the time of the project with the OECD, the SSC was barely a year old, having been implemented for the first time in 2020. Given these time constraints, the ONA has had to advance on many strategic and operational priorities in parallel, while developing the risk assessment methodology itself, as described in Chapter 1. Indeed, the SSC is not simply a risk assessment methodology. It has implications for IGAE's strategies for enhancing data governance and its own capacities for data-driven monitoring, as well as its approach to communication and co-ordination.

This chapter builds on the background and recommendations for the ONA in chapter 1 that focused on the risk assessment process, and it considers other aspects and challenges related to the SSC. It shares experiences from Turkey, Austria, Italy and Canada to support the ONA in addressing these issues. In particular, the chapter discusses issues and opportunities for enhancing the ONA's continuous supervision strategy and capacity, including recommendations for:

- institutionalising feedback loops to ensure continuous improvement to the SSC, as well as considering further automation and the use of dashboards
- taking additional steps to assess data quality with respect to the SSC
- improving the tracking of conclusions and recommendations from its continuous supervision activities
- enhancing the SSC by further investing in the ONA's capacity and specialised data skills in the continuous supervision context.

Beyond the methodology and the processes for implementing the SSC, other considerations can have an impact on the effectiveness and relevance of continuous supervision in Spain. These issues and challenges broadly reflect notions of transparency, communication and co-ordination. This section in the chapter draws inspiration from the Institute of Internal Auditors as well as supreme audit institutions, and encourages the IGAE to consider:

- improving the transparency of the SSC, including publishing the annual report and establishing audit committees
- enhancing co-ordination with key oversight institutions to ensure the effectiveness of the SSC and avoid duplication
- further developing its communication strategy to demonstrate the value of the SSC to government entities and oversight bodies.

The issues presented in the chapter are not exhaustive, but they represent some of the most immediate challenges facing the IGAE and the ONA as they advance the SSC. Addressing these issues can help to position the IGAE and the ONA to take advantage of the digital transformation that is underway in Spain's government and society. Subsequent versions of the SSC can be a driver and example for the IGAE's own modernisation in a digital age.

Enhancing strategies and capacity for data-driven monitoring

The IGAE could institutionalise feedback loops to ensure continuous improvement to the SSC, including consideration of further automation and the use of dashboards

The ONA and the IGAE's Office of Finance and Information Technology (*Oficina de Informática Presupuestaria*, OIP) developed the analytics tool that supports the SSC using internal personnel and native infrastructure. The ONA and OIP designed and developed the first version of the tool, currently in use, in 2018. The following year it was used for the first time to collect and report on information and data from self-assessment questionnaires and accounts of public entities. The year 2020 marks only the second year the ONA has used the tool for continuous supervision.

As noted, for efficiency and in accordance with the Directive, the tool itself relies on existing interactive web applications (*CICEP.red and RED.coa*) that allow public entities to send information concerning their financial and accounts data to the IGAE. The OIP developed both applications in-house using Microsoft.NET and JavaScript as a programming framework. The data from *CICEP.red and RED.coa*, along with the self-assessment questionnaires, are merged into an SQL database ("El Cubo") using Microsoft Power BI for extracting, transforming and loading (i.e. ETL processes) as well as reporting.[2] The output of this process is an Excel spreadsheet with various worksheets that summarise the information. The ONA can continue to access the detailed questionnaires and files through the CICEP.red and RED.coa. The SSC simplifies the work of ONA analysts; however, there are opportunities for further efficiencies.

While the tool has been piloted and is in use for a full financial reporting cycle, the ONA indicated that elements of the SSC strategy related to automation are still being implemented (OECD, 2020[2]). Desired criteria for the analytics tool included importing data from IGAE's internal systems and executing a risk-based analysis to identify high-risk entities. However, at this stage, the tool has only partially automated the process. Specifically, the collection of responses to self-assessment questionnaires as well as the financial indicators are fully automated, but the collection of data to assess "other qualitative risk factors" is only partially automated. Moreover, the ONA captures data in a complex series of Excel spreadsheets, and analysts manually perform the risk assessment to select entities for a further control review (ONA, 2020[3]). The risk assessment tool itself is essentially a data repository, with limited analytical functionality. The ONA also envisages using the tool to automate the evaluation reports for the entities selected for further review and in the annual reporting of results to the Ministry of Finance.

Having completed one full cycle of the SSC, the ONA could create an internal feedback loop between the OIP developers and ONA analysts as a mechanism to begin systematically monitoring the most challenging, time-consuming, and potentially error-prone aspects of the current process on an ongoing and iterative basis. In the short-term, this feedback loop could include an assessment of the need and options to adapt indicators that are partially-automated, as these have the highest likelihood of creating additional burden for analysts during the data collection phase. For continuous improvement of the SSC, the feedback loop can be institutionalised with both formal and informal channels of communication. In addition, as part of this process, the ONA could consider how statistical software, risk dashboards and other visualisation tools can support analysis, relieving some of the burden on analysts who now analyse over 420 entities using "dynamic" pivot tables in Excel to calculate ratios.

Box 2.1 presents the experience of the Turkish Court of Accounts (TCA) for assessing financial risks in municipalities. TCA created a business intelligence system called "VERA," which uses data visualisations to facilitate the identification of risks. VERA relies on a robust web-based, centralised system (Oracle Business Intelligence Enterprise) that is customisable and allows for a secure connection, even when auditors are working remotely. In addition to risk analyses for municipalities, the system allows for analysis of financial statements, accounting entries and salaries. It also supports data verification. This includes analysis of the reliability of financial and accounting data. All data that VERA collates for analysis is facilitated by different public financial management systems and data warehouses that provide the critical infrastructure for the collection, processing and reuse of data. TCA institutionalised its own feedback loop by creating a "Data Analysis Group."

Box 2.1. Turkish Court of Accounts Data Analysis System (VERA) for monitoring financial risks

In 2017, the Turkish Court of Accounts (TCA) created a "Data Analysis Group" to design methodologies for using computer-assisted audit techniques (CAAT) and enhance the capability of the TCA to assess risks in municipalities. The group had other aims, including decreasing auditors' workload, analysing big data, identifying mistakes and errors in data processing, and automation of analyses to facilitate continuous monitoring. Their efforts resulted in "VERA", TCA's Data Analysis and Business Intelligence System.

VERA provides auditees a standard, automated tool for risk-based ranking of over 1 400 municipalities. VERA allows management to take into account risks before the TCA's annual audit programming and supports the creation of the audit strategy. In addition, auditors use the results of the risk analyses to plan audits, as well as identify possible material misstatements in financial reports that could represent errors and fraud. All auditors have access to VERA, and are able to assess the results of VERA's automated analyses related to risks and financial indicators in a dashboard or automatically generated reports.

Risk profiles for municipalities reflect budget size, investments, incomes, transaction numbers and volumes, size of their expenses and demographics. Scoring of individual risks generally follows a 5 point scale. For instance, VERA assesses municipal data for liabilities and calculates debt to assets ratios. VERA assigns municipalities with the highest ratios (i.e. the highest financial risk) a score of 5.

Source: OECD Interview with TCA officials and TCA presentation.

There is a cost-benefit trade-off when investing in analytics tools for public sector entities. New systems can be costly, both in terms of the outlay in public funds to install and maintain them as well as in the time to train staff on how to use the new tools to realise the expected benefits. Moreover, the cybersecurity risks associated with using free or open source platforms or statistical software packages are particularly heightened given the privacy and ethical concerns of the types of data that public sector entities handle. However, the supreme audit institution of Austria, the Court of Audit (ACA), has successfully designed a digital tool using R, a free open source statistics package, to assess the financial risk of municipalities in the country.

Following the enlargement of its audit mandate in 2011, the ACA designed a tool to prepare a profile of each municipality (there are over 2 100) using indicators to assess financial risk, and analyse the significance of the municipality from an audit perspective. The ACA found that R software was better equipped for analysing big data than Excel, was less prone to error and the R codes could be readily re-used in future evaluations, with minor adaptations. However, the learning curve for ACA analysts was significant given the level of detailed technical expertise required. Box 2.2 gives more detail on how the ACA addressed these challenges.

Box 2.2. Use of open source statistical software (R) at the Austrian Court of Audit

Since 1929, the Austrian Court of Audit (ACA) has been entitled to audit municipalities with more than 20 000 inhabitants. However, in recent years, municipalities in Austria have progressively been entrusted with more budgets to deliver services in such areas as social affairs, education and healthcare. This has resulted in an increase in the financial and economic significance of municipalities, and since 2011 the ACA has been entitled to audit those with more than 10 000 inhabitants. The extended audit responsibility has prompted the ACA to develop a tool to monitor the financial health of Austrian municipalities.

The tool operates mainly through the statistics software "R" and enables municipalities to be compared using different criteria, as well as observation of changes in municipalities and select the ones with the highest financial risk. The ACA obtains raw data from the country's statistical body. The data include detailed information on the closed accounts of the municipalities, statements of debts and liabilities, and socio-demographic data.

By ranking the municipalities according to their financial risk based on certain indicators, the tool allows the ACA to profile each of the 2 356 municipalities in Austria and to assess them with regard to their significance for the audit activities. The tool is used for audit planning and for the preparation of audits at the operational level (e.g. for the selection of peers). Upon request, the ACA also provides the relevant fact sheets to the respective municipalities.

Source: OECD interview of ACA officials and OECD (2020[4]), *Auditing Decentralised Policies in Brazil: Collaborative and Evidence-Based Approaches for Better Outcomes*, OECD Publishing, Paris.

Improvements to the SSC concerning IT, data and tools do not occur in isolation of IGAE's broader IT environment or digitalisation strategy. Legacy technology and capability gaps are often obstacles to digital transformation in the public sector. The OIP team designing the SSC tool were limited to building a tool from existing in-house systems at the IGAE. The process began with *CICEP.red* and *RED.coa* and OIP indicated that data sources will be expanded to include other systems such as CINCO.net (for budget and accounting data) and AUDI.net (for audit and internal control reports etc.). Taking advantage of the introduction of the momentum surrounding the pilot phase, the OIP and the ONA could use the SSC as a catalyst for making more systemic advancements to the broader digitalisation strategy of the IGAE. This could include strengthening key elements that have direct implications for the SSC, such as the data strategy, data management and automation of analysis, as well as IGAE's oversight and control activities more broadly. From an institutional perspective, it could also include an assessment of the Enterprise Architecture (EA) of the IGAE.

EA is a practice that focuses on the alignment of an entities strategy and the IT infrastructure it has to achieve goals and objectives (Canada Border Services Agency, 2019[5]). It guides the process of planning and designing IT capabilities to meet objectives. EA defines the current- and target-state architectures, aligning with the entity's strategy, priorities, and IT assets and capabilities (Canada Border Services Agency, 2019[5]). Contemporary approaches to EA go beyond a focus on improving processes to include a consideration of outcomes. The early stages of the SSC provides a concrete application for considering IGAE's EA in a broader context and promoting further digitalisation in the coming years. Box 2.3 provides some insights from the internal audit function in the Canadian Border Services Agency and its review of the EA Programme.

Box 2.3. Auditing of Enterprise Architecture of the Canadian Border Services Agency

In 2009, the Canadian Border Services Agency (CBSA) created an Enterprise Architecture (EA) Programme to align its strategy with its IT Infrastructure. The EA Programme has a dedicated team, CBSA's Enterprise Architecture Division (EAD), which is responsible for delivering and managing the programme. As an entity-wide programme, stakeholders include all CBSA Branches. The EA Programme adopted the Open Group Architecture Framework (TOGAF), a generally-accepted framework for enterprise architecture. The framework provides guidelines for the successful development and execution of an EA Programme strategy.

According to the internal audit (IA) function of the CBSA, the EA Programme can play a significantrole to ensure that   Information Management/Information Technology (IM/IT) tools   and capabilities are aligned with the overall strategy of the CBSA and the Government of Canada (GC). "An effective EA Programme should result in efficiencies and cost savings through the reuse of shared services, elimination of redundant operations, and optimisation of service delivery through the streamlining of business processes, data standardisation and systems integration."

The objective of the audit was to assess whether the CBSA established an EA Programme that adds value, is effectively governed and is aligned with the CBSA's current needs and priorities and the future direction of the CBSA.

The CBSA's IA function conducted in audit in 2019 that focused on the activities of the EA Programme during the period between April 1, 2017 and March 31, 2019, including an examination of the following:

- CBSA governance processes, including architectural governance processes, to support adoption of the EA Programme within the CBSA.

- The adoption of EA solutions by the CBSA for business processes and transformational activities.

- Performance measurement and reporting for the EA Programme.

The IA function found that the CBSA established an EA Programme that is aligned with the objectives and priorities of the Government of Canada and the CBSA itself. However, it identified key areas for improvement of the EA Programme to enhance its value for the CBSA. Key findings of the audit included:

- Governance committees are active in fulfilling their responsibilities related to the EA; however, there was a need for an Architecture Review Board (ARB) to regularly discuss architecture issues and oversee the governance of "architecture variances.

- There is a need for more systematic ongoing review processes and communication of EA artefacts to all stakeholders.

- Embed EA considerations early in planning processes to enhance uptake of solutions. The IA function found that the EAD was generally consulted, as required, for IT-enabled projects, but there was no process to consult EAD for non-IT enabled projects.

- Governance processes were inadequate for holding individuals accountable for non-compliance CBSA's approved EA standards governance.

- Performance measures for the EA Programme were not established or tracked.

The IA function's audit underscored the need for improving the EA programme so that it added value to the agency. It also noted the risks for the CBSA in implementing solutions that are counter to the EA programme. Specifically, it could result in bypassing requirements for security, privacy, interoperability, accessibility and open information, as well as a lost opportunity for costs avoidance and efficiencies.

Source: (Canada Border Services Agency, 2019[5]).

Assessing the IGAE's EA was beyond the scope of this project. Many resources that offer frameworks to support the IGAE in this assessment are decades old, but are still based on fundamental principles and practices that are relevant today. For instance, the IGAE may draw inspiration for assessing its own EA from the U.S, Government Accountability Office's *Organizational Transformation: A Framework for Assessing and Improving EA Management* (US Government Accountability Office, 2017[6]). This framework draws from an even older source, *Information Technology Investment Management: A Framework for Assessing and Improving Process Maturity* (US Government Accountability Office, 2004[7]). These frameworks offer tools and insights to inform IGAE's assessment of its own digitalisation strategy.

The IGAE could take additional steps to assess data quality with respect to the SSC

Spain is among the vanguard of countries that have embraced a digital government approach, employing digital tools and information technology to modernise public administration and deliver better policies and public services.[3] This long-standing commitment to harnessing the benefits of technology is reflected in Spain's top ten ranking in the OECD's Digital Government Index 2019 (OECD, 2020[8]). Governments are increasingly embracing a data-driven approach are leveraging technology to not only achieve cost-savings and administrative efficiencies but as a tool to inform managerial decision making and take preventive actions to respond to risks. Moreover, international standards have evolved to reflect the emergence of a public sector that is data-driven and risk-based. For example, OECD instruments and standards recognise the added value of investment in developing effective data policies, data governance models, skills and capacity (OECD, 2019[9]).

Deriving meaning from data through analytical tools or techniques, commonly referred to as "data analytics", has been transformational for public sector entities who apply this approach in service delivery and design, monitoring and evaluation of the performance of programmes and policies or for oversight purposes (Fazekas, M., Ugale, G, & Zhao, A., 2019[10]). While data analytics can be applied in diverse ways, there are common principles and practices to maximise its effectiveness that are relevant in multiple contexts. These include having a strategy for analytics with clearly defined objective, as well as ensuring effective institutional and data governance, technology, people and skills, and project-level planning.

Data governance includes standards and controls to help ensure availability, consistency, security and integrity of data. The IGAE applies European and national data protection and information security regulations in its use of data and digital tools (OECD, 2020[2]). While data for the indicators and ratios in the automated reviews of the SSC is captured from the financial reporting systems, the IGAE indicated that it does not perform independent systems audits or edit checks to verify the reliability of data. In addition, the ONA relies on attestations from senior management at the relevant entity regarding the accuracy and validity of the data reported. Officials said the control reviews provide an opportunity for following up on any questions regarding the data, but at this point the entity has already been selected for review.

Given the weighting of 40% assigned to the responses of the self-assessment questionnaires in the preliminary risk assessment, validation or at least some corroboration of this data is vital. IGAE could develop a plan to improve data validation and corroboration of self-reported data as part of its data quality management process, including spot-checking and formalised guidance for analysts to ensure systematic checking of facts during control reviews. Table 2.1 shows the European Commission's good practices on data quality management, which the IGAE could consider as part of future efforts to ensure data quality.

Table 2.1. European Commission's Data Quality Management Process

Data quality management process
Define data quality: define the quality components and standards.
Plan and implement: develop and implement a set of procedures to produce, check, and ensure data of acceptable quality.
Perform acceptance tests and evaluate results: perform tests to compare delivered data to acceptability metrics.
Take corrective action: take steps to clean, correct, re-collect or reprocess data as needed to achieve data acceptance standards.
Report on data quality: document the data quality standards, protocols, processing methods, acceptance tests, and results. Report inappropriate data records to the data source holder, who is expected to take action in correct it.
Improve the process: use the knowledge and experience gained to modify processes as needed to improve data quality.

Source: (European Platform Undeclared Work, 2016[11]).

The ONA could improve its tracking of conclusions and recommendations from its continuous supervision activities

Having piloted the SSC in 2019, the ONA can consider additional measures to monitor and track the status of recommendations it makes. As discussed, the ONA's conclusions following its control reviews, which it documents in an evaluation report, can include one of three actions: maintain, merge or dissolve. When the ONA's determination is to maintain an entity, it may also provide management with recommendations for improvements that it can make to its policies and processes. For instance, the ONA may recommend that the entity prepare strategic planning documents in accordance with the Public Administration Legal Regulation Act of 2015 (*Ley 40/2015 de 1 de octubre de Régimen Jurídico del Sector Público*), or to further specify the activities and functions the entity performs.

As of March 2020, the ONA had begun monitoring the extent to which entities had implemented its recommendations made following the control reviews in 2019. The ONA conducts monitoring by means of a letter that it sends to the line ministry of the audited entity. Through this letter, the ONA requests information that describes the progress the entity has made in implementing recommendations the ONA has made. The monitoring focuses on recommendation that managers of the audited body had previously accepted in response to the provisional report or the audited entity's own ministry. However, audited entities may disagree with the ONA's recommendations, in which case the Ministry of Finance makes a decision to accept or reject the recommendation. There is currently no mechanism in place to track the decision of the Ministry of Finance when the ONA and the audited entity disagree on recommendations.

In addition, the ONA can improve its processes for tracking if and how the Council of Ministers acts on its recommendations. The SSC is a tool that informs decisions of policymakers. Decision to dissolve or merge entities are highly political, and in some cases, policymakers decide not to adopt the measures that the ONA recommends. This phase of decision-making is opaque. Once the ONA sends the evaluation report, A formal mechanism to track and communicate the judgement and actions of the Ministry of Finance and the Council of Ministers does not exist. As a result, the ONA does not know how policymakers use and act on its evaluation reports.

International auditing standards call for audit institutions to follow-up on audit recommendations as a critical element for enhancing the impact of their reports. "Follow-up is a process by which internal auditors evaluate the adequacy, effectiveness, and timeliness of actions taken by management on reported observations and recommendations," as well as whether management or the Board has assumed the risk of not taking actions (The Institute of Internal Auditors, 2009[12]). Systematic tracking and monitoring of the uptake of recommendations facilitates effective follow-up. As discussed, in Spain, the ONA and SSC stakeholders, including the Ministry of Finance, could improve two types of follow-up and tracking mechanisms. They include: 1) processes for tracking recommendations for audited entities in relation to its control/evaluation reports, including the Ministry of Finance's judgement when the ONA and the audited entity disagree; and 2) tracking decisions made or actions not taken by policymakers in response to its evaluations reports.

Recommendation tracking can take many forms, including online and internal databases, as well as narrative reports that summarise recommendations. The aforementioned work of the US Government Accountability Office's to assess duplication, fragmentation and overlap in government offers an example of an online tracker for recommendations. The Action Tracker is an online tool that tracks the progress made by both the Congress and federal agencies in response to GAO's recommendations to reduce duplication, fragmentation and overlap. The categorisation of the status of recommendations includes: *New-Pending, Not Addressed, Partially Addressed, Addressed, Consolidate or Other, and Closed-Not Addressed* (US Goverment Accountability Office, 2021[13]). The recommendations can be downloaded in *XLSX* or *CSV* formats, thereby promoting greater public use, analysis and awareness of its work.

For policymakers and decision-making bodies, such as the Council of Ministers in Spain, the narrative around recommendation tracking can be a useful input for understanding the nature of recommendations and impact of action or inaction. A narrative can provide the context to complement a status list of recommendations. As noted by the Institute of Internal Auditors (IIA) in its White Paper, *Reporting on the Status of Audit Recommendations*, narrative reports are particularly beneficial for audit committees, if Spain were to develop these, as described in the next section. Table 2.2 provides considerations for the ONA to consider in terms of the style and focus of such reports, contrasting what the IIA sees as low-value versus high-value narrative reporting styles. recognising that any narratives on recommendation tracking would need tailoring to ONA's context, and potentially integrated with existing reports that result from the SSC.

Table 2.2. Reporting styles for follow-up of audit recommendations

Element	Low-Value	High-Value
Report style	List of all audit recommendations.	A report on open recommendations that tells a story and has analysis.
Approach	• Obtain updates from management and update the recommendations database. • Print list of: all audit recommendations with their status, or; all open recommendations with their status.	• Obtain updates from management and update the recommendations database. • Download and analyse the data for trends and prepare relevant graphs. • Discern the 'story' of how well recommendations are being addressed by management and prepare appropriate narrative.
Content	• Short covering paper; essentially we are required to follow-up recommendations under auditing standards; here is a list of all the audit recommendations. • List of recommendations with their status.	• Opinion on management's overall level of commitment to addressing agreed audit recommendations. • Commentary on at risk recommendations, including their original and revised targeted completion dates and comments on action in train. • Trends (3 to 5 years) of actions opened, closed, overdue, and total number of actions currently open. • Trends and / graphs on recommendations being raised applied against different business risk categories. • Graphs illustrating through different lenses overdue recommendations, such as: risk ratings; ageing of periods overdue; business area; and list of open recommendations (in full or part) as an attachment.
Impact	Low. Meets the basic requirements of the audit committee.	High. In addition to meeting the basic requirements, this reporting type helps to provide risk-based and objective assurance, advice and insights.

Source: Adapted from (The Institute of Internal Auditors Australia, 2020[14]).

The IGAE could enhance the SSC by further investing in the ONA's capacity and specialised data skills in the continuous supervision context

The IGAE—specifically, a small team in the ONA and the OIP—absorbed the responsibilities of the SSC as a result of the CORA reform proposals and the Public Administration Legal Regulation Act of 2015. The design, implementation and continuous improvement to the SSC and supervision of 420 public entities creates a demand on internal resources that did not exist prior to the reforms. Moreover, in response to the OECD's questionnaire, officials of the ONA highlighted the increase in workload from the SSC, coupled with the need for further specialisation. To ensure the ONA can effectively deliver its SSC mandate, the IGAE and the ONA could consider establishing a dedicated team or unit within the ONA. This team could consist of a multi-disciplinary group of experts, including auditors and data experts, who could address the demands of the SSC as a unique work stream in the ONA.

The ONA could take inspiration from other audit entities that recognised the need for a dedicated workforce to develop data-driven risk assessments. For instance, in the aforementioned example from the Turkish Court of Accounts (TCA), the TCA created a "Data Analysis Group" to design methodologies for using computer-assisted audit techniques. In Italy, the Court of Audit harnessed the expertise of a cross-functional team of auditors and technicians to deliver on its own monitoring and oversight activities, called the "Data Analysis Competency Centre" (see Box 2.4). The ONA could contemplate in more detail how best to develop and structure its team as part of its efforts for taking a strategic approach to digitalisation and assessing its Enterprise Architecture, as previously described. The ONA may also consider targeted training programmes for OIP data technicians and ONA analysts to expand their skillsets, as well as recruitment targeting new staff with the requisite data or analytical skills.

Box 2.4. Data-driven monitoring and supervision at the Italian Court of Audit

The digital strategy of the Italian Court of Audit (Corte dei Conti, CdC) focuses on three main areas: knowledge sharing and data integration; its business intelligence system (called ConosCo); and digitalisation. ConosCo supports the CdC's mandate to monitor public finances and expenditures and enhance reports to Parliament. The CdC launched ConosCo in 2008 as a set of methodologies, processes, architectures, and technologies to transform raw data into meaningful and information for decision-making and control purposes. The tool is not meant for risk-based audit selection, which is a process that is primarily used for the CdC's performance auditing portfolio.

ConosCo relies on financial data sources from both central and local governments, as well as external parties like the European Commission, which feed into a data warehouse and is then transmitted to dashboards for auditors to use during the audit process. For instance, member states of the European Union (EU) are required to communicate to the Irregularities Management System (IMS) of the European Anti-Fraud Office (OLAF) any fraud and irregularities over EUR 10 000 related to European Union funds. The CdC is able to access this data through one of its own systems, and through ConosCo, make this information available to auditors and regional offices. The dashboards available to auditors in ConosCo support the analysis of indicators for detecting fraud and irregularities, as well as broader issues for monitoring the financial performance of government entities.

According to CdC officials, key features that enable the Court to carry out its function include:

- Clear objectives to drive the activities related to ConosCo.
- Access to reliable and trustworthy data at national and regional levels. Memorandums of Understandings with key ministries facilitate this access.
- A level of automation that reflects the standard architecture of a data warehouse with requirements adjusted to meet the needs of the end users.

- Automation that allows for regular reporting, based on reporting requirements found in laws and regulations.
- The right mix of software, tailored to the CdC, including Microsoft Strategy, Power BI and visualisation to aid users in understanding the data and quickly drawing insights or create reports.

In addition, the CdC developed a "Data Analysis Competency Centre," which is a new cross-functional team that brings together business and technical competencies to support the effective implementation of ConosCo. The Centre will support users of ConosCo to make better decision using machine learning, analytics, predictive analysis and other data analytics techniques. At the time of writing this report, this Centre is still in development and intends to be a multi-disciplinary team with knowledge and skills that span levels of government (i.e. national and regional) as well as technologies. According to CdC officials, this effort signals a recognition that any data-driven tool is not static, and requires a capacity-building strategy to support its development and evolution.

Source: OECD interview with CdC officials.

Improving transparency, communication and co-ordination

The IGAE could take steps to improve the transparency of the SSC, including publishing the annual report and establishing audit committees.

The Open Budget Survey (OBS) for 2019, the most recent year available, measures three key areas of governance: transparency, public participation and budget oversight. Transparency metrics in the OBS focus on public access to information as to how the government raises and spends public resources (International Budget Partnership, 2019[15]). According to the International Budget Partnership (IBP), a transparency score of at least 61 out of 100 indicates a country is "likely publishing enough material to support informed public debate on the budget.[4] Spain's score for 2019 was 53, as shown in Figure 2.1.

Figure 2.1. Transparency score for Spain in the 2019 Open Budget Survey

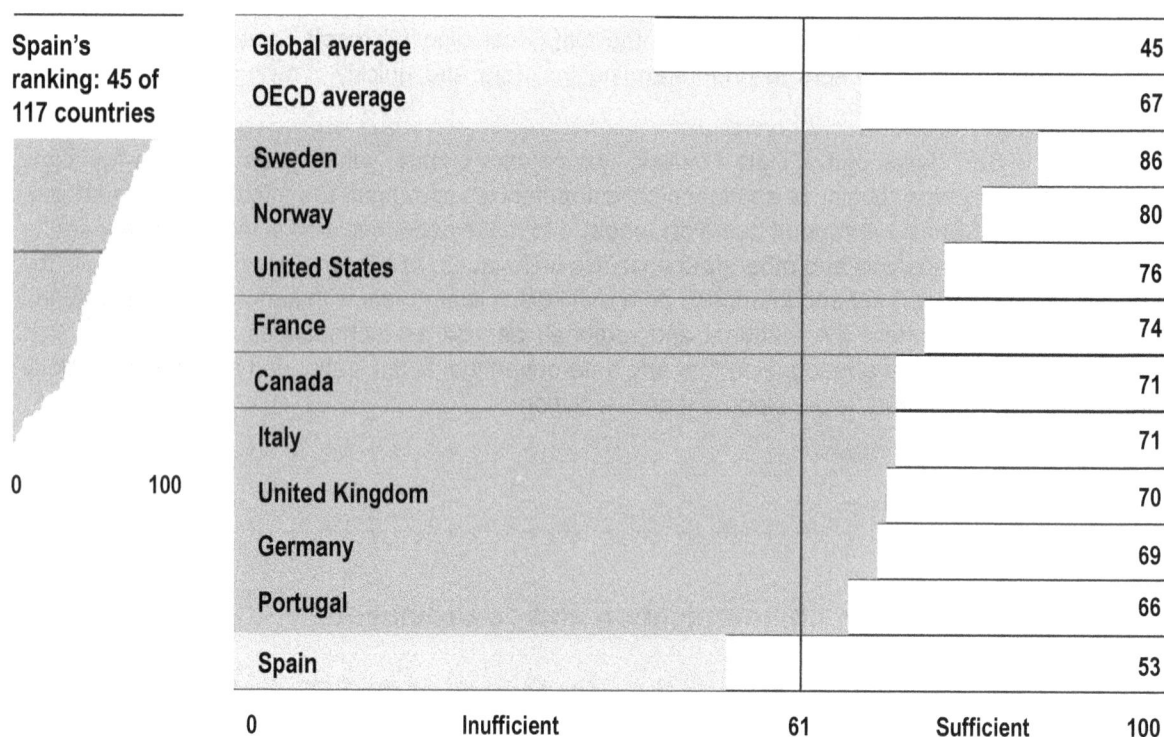

Spain's ranking: 45 of 117 countries

0   100

	Score
Global average	45
OECD average	67
Sweden	86
Norway	80
United States	76
France	74
Canada	71
Italy	71
United Kingdom	70
Germany	69
Portugal	66
Spain	53

0   Insufficient   61   Sufficient   100

Source: (International Budget Partnership, 2019[15])

The OBS also covers questions related to budget oversight, and concerning questions related to audit oversight, Spain scores comparatively well (95 out of 100). However, specific questions provide further context that are relevant for the IGAE and accountability actors as key standard-bearers for the state of transparency in the Spanish government. In particular, when asked, "Does the executive make available to the public a report on what steps it has taken to address audit recommendations or findings that indicate a need for remedial action?," the response was the same as many OECD member countries and others OBS surveyed. "No, the executive does not report on steps it has taken to address audit findings." (International Budget Partnership, 2019[15]).

Against this backdrop, the IGAE can help to enhance transparency in government and meet public demand by making public its annual reports from the SSC. This is particularly critical given the greater attention to the effectiveness, efficiency and economy of government in the wake of the COVID-19 pandemic and increased public spending. IGAE officials are required to maintain confidentiality regarding control activities (Government of Spain, 2003[16]); however, exceptions are made in related laws, such as the possibility for public investigative bodies to publish summary reports about their activities (Government of Spain, 2019[17]). Although it follows separate standards for supreme audit institutions, the Spanish Court of Accounts has the power and mandate to publish its reports and audit findings. To ensure such transparency, the IGAE and the ONA could identify and make use of existing legal exceptions to share the results of the SSC externally. At a minimum, while respecting its requirements of confidentiality, this could include making summary reports of key findings and recommendations that stem from the SSC accessible to other oversight bodies. According to ONA officials, key stakeholders with whom it could share its reports from continuous supervision include:

- The Court of Auditors to support its external control activities of the economic-financial management of the public sector.

- The General Directorate of Budgets to inform processes and discussions for determining the state budget and allocating resources.
- The General Inspections of Services within line ministries to improve its control activities.
- Other relevant entities, such as the Independent Authority for Spanish Fiscal Responsibility, an entity responsible for fiscal control (*La Autoridad Independiente de Responsabilidad Fiscal*, AIREF).

Sharing the results of the SSC more broadly could have broader implications for transparency of internal audit and IGAE's work in general. This would promote good practices for reporting transparency within the Spanish administration, and further align the IGAE with international standards for publishing reports. Box 2.5 provides context on reporting transparency in the internal audit context, drawing from a seminal publication and survey data of the Institute of Internal Auditors. In many countries, publishing internal audit reports has been a long-established practice.

Box 2.5. Survey of the Institute of Internal Auditor's on audit report transparency in the public sector

The Institute of Internal Auditors (IIA) conducted a study to identify global internal audit report transparency practices in the public sector, and help public sector internal auditors and decision makers benchmark transparency practices. The IIA's International Standards for the Professional Practice of Internal Auditing (Standards)—Standard 2440: Disseminating Results—notes that the chief audit executive "must communicate results to the appropriate parties."

In 2012, the IIA Public Sector Committee surveyed internal audit entities in the public sector to obtain information about their reporting transparency practices. The Committee received 160 responses for a survey that was a combination of 17 multiple-choice and open-ended questions. The survey respondents represented 14 countries across five continents. Bearing in mind that the survey was conducted in December 2012, some of the key findings still have relevance for Spain today given the current state of transparency per the Open Budget Survey and the relevance to recommendations in this report:

- Most of the public sector entities disseminate the internal audit report to an audit committee or senior management.
- Federal/national governments are less likely than lower levels of government to disseminate internal audit reports to internal parties, including impacted management, except to the board or audit committee.
- Most entities disseminate reports to external auditors.
- All entities that disseminate internal audit reports to an external party also disseminate these reports to senior management and/or legal counsel.
- Entities that are subject to public information laws are more transparent in the publication of the internal audit report.

The IIA asked respondents about the internal and external recipients of surveys. Of the 146 respondents that answered the question concerning internal dissemination of reports, 102 (70%) indicated that the internal audit report is disseminated to the board or audit committee, 93 (64%) to the executive director or president and 81 (55%) to impacted management. Regarding external dissemination of reports, 129 respondents answered the question and stated the supreme audit institution (61%), legislative auditor (22%), legislature/Parliament (22%) and the comptroller/Treasurer (14%) and other (19%), were among the main external recipients of the internal audit report.

Source: (The Institute of Internal Auditors, 2017[18]) and (The Institute of internal Auditors, 2012[19]).

The IGAE faces more systemic, broader capacity issue to ensure that recommendations and results of the SSC are monitored and that stakeholders have shared priorities for supervision. The tracking system and follow-up reporting described above are critical mechanisms to promote accountability and transparency, but they are technical means for managing operations and informing stakeholders. The IGAE could benefit from mechanisms that also convene relevant stakeholders and promote co-ordination. There are several modalities to accomplish this. The first step is for the IGAE to clarify its objectives in this regard, and then decide on the form, function and stakeholders. In particular, an objective to engage formally and frequently with political actors and key decision-makers of the SSC, such as the Council of Ministers, can lead to a different co-ordination mechanism than an objective that is more technical in nature, such as involving audit subjects to ensure the uptake of IGAE's recommendations within ministries.

Depending on the ultimate objective, one option is for the IGAE to establish a working group of oversight bodies, including those listed above, with a mandate to support the delivery, improvement and dissemination of results from continuous supervision. In the short-term, this would be the most effective and efficient way for the IGAE to advance constructive partnerships and information sharing in the context of the SSC. As a more robust, formal mechanism, the IGAE could consider taking the lead on the establishment of an audit committee(s) within the Ministry of Finance (and/or across Ministries) to bolster co-ordination during the next phase of developing the SSC.

In the public sector, independent audit committees are board-level committees with a majority of independent member charged with providing oversight of management practices in key governance areas (The Institute of Internal Auditors, 2014[20]). Audit committees have a mutually beneficial relationship with internal audit, as they hold management accountable for assessing and implementing, where appropriate, internal audit recommendations (The Institute of Internal Auditors Australia, 2020[14]). Audit committees can help to define priorities, promote the flow of information and insights between different stakeholders and advise on the adequacy of resources. Audit committees can add value to an entity in other ways, including:

- Facilitate well-informed, efficient, and effective decision-making.
- Promote and monitor an ethical culture.
- Ensure compliance with a well-designed code of conduct.
- Oversee an effective system of risk oversight and management.
- Oversee an effective and efficient internal control system.
- Oversee internal and external reporting of financial and nonfinancial information.
- Promote effective communication with audit activity and external assurance providers and respond appropriately to matters they raise (The Institute of Internal Auditors, 2014[20]).

In Spain, public sector audit committees are rare. There is no legal requirement for public entities to establish an audit committee, except for state mercantile companies (The European Confederation of Institutes of Internal Auditing, 2019[21]). The Good Governance Code addresses listed companies but it does not affect public sector entities, which can voluntarily set up an audit committee. While not legally obligated to do so, the IGAE could consider spearheading the development of an audit committee that would have the SSC as part of its responsibilities. The audit committee could be made up of internal stakeholders in the Ministry of Finance, Council of Ministers and other oversight bodies, as well as the General Inspection of Service, among others. It could provide a forum for sharing the results of the SSC and support improvements in the future. The mandate of any audit committee could be broader than the SSC, and would be informed by existing laws, regulations and policies. An audit committee charter would define its mandate and establish its authority with respect to its activities.

The IGAE could enhance co-ordination with key oversight institutions to ensure the effectiveness of the SSC and avoid duplication

To perform continuous supervision, the IGAE is legally mandated to leverage available financial and economic data, information provided by the entities to comply with the new requirements and recommendations of the Inspector General of Services within the line ministries (Government of Spain, 2018[22]). Similar to countries such as France, Spain has Inspectors General of Services whose role as internal audit functions involves reviewing services and entities affiliated with the relevant ministry and making proposals to improve and simplify administrative procedures. This role also encompasses reviews of services for quality assurance purposes, effectiveness and value for money[5] (OECD, 2014[1]).

The role of the Inspectors General was also expanded under the Public Administration Legal Regulation Act. It now includes an effectiveness control (*control de eficacia*), which is an assessment of the extent to which an entity has met its objectives and evaluates the use of its resources in line with its strategic action plan (Government of Spain, 2015[23]).[6] The IGAE indicated that the effectiveness control complements the continuous supervision process, with the work of the Inspectors General serving as inputs to the evaluation of the entity's rationality (*racionalidad)*.

As summarised in Table 2.3, co-ordination is one of the guiding principles for effective continuous supervision stated in the SSC Directive. The Inspectors General can co-ordinate their effectiveness control activities with the IGAE and establish a channel of communication with the oversight bodies of the entities subject to supervision. Putting this principle into practice, the IGAE has met periodically with the Inspector General of the Ministry of Finance to raise awareness of the model of continuous supervision. It has also collaborated on a guide for Inspector General of Services performing the effectiveness control with the Directorate General of Public Governance within the Ministry of Public Administration and Civil Service (OECD, 2020[2]). This guide incorporates elements related to continuous supervision for inspectors to consider as they conduct effectiveness control reviews.

Table 2.3. Co-ordination is one of the guiding principles of Spain's continuous supervision system

Principle	Description
Autonomy and independence	Activities are carried out by civil servants who are functionally independent of the management of the entities subject to continuous supervision activity.
Co-ordination	As it is a horizontal system, a channel of communication must be established with the bodies that oversee the entities subject to continuous supervision. In particular, co-ordination of continuous supervision with the effectiveness control performed by the Inspector General of Services is required. For state trading companies, communication with the shareholders is also required.
Efficiency	Activities contribute to the efficient use of public resources, as the objective of the continuous supervision system is to analyse and evaluate the validity of the circumstances underlying the establishment of public sector institutions.
Right to contradict	Before the conclusions and recommendations of continuous supervision are finalised, the entity being supervised and its oversight body are guaranteed time to respond to the observations.

Note: Article 5, Guiding Principles of the System *Principios orientadores del Sistema.*
Source: *Ministerio de Hacienda y Función Pública* (Government of Spain, 2018[22]).

In keeping with the guiding principle on co-ordination stipulated in the Directive for performing continuous supervision (Government of Spain, 2018[22]), the ONA planned a series of activities to raise awareness of the SSC with other control and oversight bodies. This included clarifying roles and responsibilities of the IGAE vis-à-vis the Inspectors General of Services and bodies supervising the public sector entities (*órganos de tutela*), as well as building relationships with these bodies to support effective delivery of the SSC (ONA, 2018[24]).

IGAE applies International Auditing Standards adapted to the Spanish public sector. In line with ISA 610 and NIA-ES-SP 1610, the ONA must evaluate the objectivity and competency of the work of the internal audit function, the Inspectors General of Services, before it uses it (International Auditing and Assurance Standards Board, 2013[25]; IGAE, 2019[26]). While such safeguards are critical, international good practice on internal auditing in the public sector also recommends information sharing, co-ordination of activities and even reliance by internal audit functions on the work of other assurance providers depending on the circumstances (The Institute of Internal Auditors, 2019[27]). This co-ordination can be particularly advantageous when resources are limited for all parties involved, including the entity being reviewed. This guidance to internal auditors explicitly recognises the integral role that inspectors and external auditors play in public sector oversight.

The mandates of the audit and control bodies in Spain are defined in law, and current regulation does not allow for information exchange between them. The ONA therefore currently has informal communication channels with other oversight bodies. For example, it shares planned public audit activities with the Tribunal de Cuentas in advance of the plans being approved to minimise duplication or overburdening of public sector entities.[7] From interviews with the Inspector General of Services, while co-ordination of control activities with the ONA occurs, this is on an informal basis (OECD, 2020[28]). A provision to facilitate information exchange between the internal and external audit bodies was submitted and approved in 2020 as a modification of the 2003 General Budgetary Law (Government of Spain, 2003[16]).

However, in the absence of audit committees or other forms of intra- and inter-ministerial co-ordination, there are opportunities for the audit bodies to improve sharing of relevant risk information generated for or as a result of the SSC, without impeding their autonomy or independence. Closer co-ordination between the internal audit, external audit institutions and other assurance providers is crucial for achieving the following complementary objectives:

- exchanging information, audit plans and reports between the internal auditors and the SAI, to help conduct audits, including evaluations of the effectiveness of internal control and risk-management arrangements
- achieving economies of scale as audit entities co-operate on methodological and training matters
- SAIs advising or acting as an observer, taking part in regular meetings of the heads of internal audit units (as happens in Austria, Bulgaria, Denmark, Hungary, Latvia, Netherlands, Poland and the United Kingdom)
- streamlining interactions and communication with both external and internal audit bodies
- agreeing common standards, tools and procedures to facilitate effective co-operation.

Strengthening and formalising the co-operation and co-ordination mechanisms between the different control, internal audit and external audit institutions is crucial. Improved co-operation between internal and external control and audit institutions relies on a number of factors, first and foremost being a commitment to take an active role and the willingness to make necessary changes. Both INTOSAI and the IIA have issued international standards and guidance relating to the co-ordination and co-operation between SAIs and internal auditors in the public sector, including INTOSAI GOV 9150 *Coordination and Cooperation between SAIs and Internal Auditors in the Public Sector* (INTOSAI 2010) and IIA IPPF Standard 2050 (IIA 2016) and Practice Advisory 2050-1 *Coordination* (IIA 2009). Moreover, a paper prepared jointly by the European Entity of Supreme Audit Institutions (EUROSAI) and the European Confederation of Institutes of Internal Auditing (ECIIA) elaborates the main trends in the co-ordination between external and internal audit institutions (see Box 2.6).

Box 2.6. EUROSAI and ECIIA Study: Co-ordination between external and internal auditors

In 2014, EUROSAI and ECIIA jointly published a study that elaborated the mechanisms and challenges for co-operation and co-ordination between external and internal audit entities. The following are some of the key findings from the report:

A very large majority of SAIs are using international standards or international references regarding co-ordination and co-operation with internal audit institutions. Most of them refer in general to the International Standards for Supreme Audit Institutions (ISSAIs), International Standards on Auditing (ISA) and INTOSAI's GOV standards, such as ISSAI 1610, ISA 610, INTOSAI GOV 9140 and INTOSAI GOV 9150. Only a minority have explicit, written SAI internal rules, such as auditing manuals, standards, guidance, procedures or checklists, documenting and formalising the co-ordination and co-operation channels.

Co-ordination and co-operation between SAIs and internal auditors is often described as "informal", which can be difficult to assess or ensure the quality of its implementation. The most common benefits of co-operation and co-ordination cited include:

- promoting good governance by exchange of ideas and knowledge
- more effective and efficient audits based on a clearer understanding of the respective audit roles with better co-ordinated internal and external audit activity
- resulting from co-ordinated planning and communication
- refined audit scope for SAIs and internal auditors.

However, almost half of the responding SAIs stated they experience risks or identify potential risks in relation to co-ordination and co-operation. A majority of SAIs pursued co-ordination and co-operation largely in the following areas:

- evaluating the audited entity's internal control framework and risk-management arrangements
- evaluating the entity's compliance with laws and regulations
- documenting the entity's systems and operational processes.

Source: EUROSAI and ECIIA (2014), Coordination and Cooperation between Supreme Audit Institutions and Internal Auditors in the Public Sector.

The IGAE could further develop its communication strategy to demonstrate the value of the SSC to government entities and oversight bodies

While the SSC is a legal requirement for entities, the IGAE could benefit from adopting an approach that promotes this added value of the process to entities beyond compliance. Stakeholders from the line ministries indicated an interest in being able to discuss and share recommended good practices as a result of the SSC with peers or other government institutions. They also welcomed more informal discussions and communication with the ONA.

The Ministry of Finance reflected on the benefits to entities and affiliated line ministries in having access to the results of the risk assessment ranking in the automated review component of the SSC. This information was seen as potentially useful to entities for their own risk assessment purposes. It also provides line ministries with greater visibility on the performance of entities that are not often on the radar, even if there is no immediate concern over its financial sustainability (OECD, 2020[28]). Increased automation and real-time information were cited as areas that the ONA could improve to better support entity's efforts to provide information for the SSC (OECD, 2020[28]).

The ONA can therefore consider leveraging the broader application of the results of the SSC to promote its benefits as a valuable tool for improving the strategy setting, decision-making, and daily management and operations of public entities. Management of public entities have the primary responsibility to establish and use their internal control system to identify and effectively mitigate programme and risks (The Institute of Internal Auditors, 2019[27]). The people who are responsible for achieving the entity's objectives and delivering its services should also take responsibility over risk management, including identifying and putting in place control activities to mitigate risks. "Management ownership" implies not only that management and staff understand the institutional reform, but also that they embrace it. Sharing the results of the risk assessment component of the SSC could enable this.

As this is still a new process and a legal requirement, a learning curve for entities is to be expected. However, ONA should consider opportunities to raise awareness of the process and the expectations so that entities can better prepare and organise limited resources to respond. The ONA indicated that training on the requirements of the SSC was envisaged to be incorporated as a module on public administration training for civil servants and for new recruits to the IGAE in 2021 (OECD, 2020[2]). The ONA could consider including targeted reports of the results of the SSC that reflects the information needs of its various stakeholders where permitted by regulation.

Conclusion

In a short timeframe, the IGAE and the ONA have developed an effective methodology for continuous supervision in Spain that reflects the original spirit of the 2013 CORA reform proposals and subsequent regulations. As the ONA develops the SSC, in addition to enhancements to the risk assessment methodology described in Chapter 1, it could strengthen its strategy and capacity to make use of data and ensure that processes are in place for continuous improvement. This could include establishing feedback loops to begin systematically and iteratively monitoring the most challenging, time-consuming and error-prone aspects of the current process.

Data governance, data management and data skills are all key factors that can influence the effectiveness of the SSC. The chapter makes several recommendations and sub-recommendations for the IGAE and the ONA that touches on these areas. For instance, the chapter highlights opportunities for the ONA to automate processes for importing data and analyses, some of which are now partially automated. It also suggest that the ONA take additional steps to validate and corroborate self-reported data to provide further assurance of the quality of the data inputted into the SSC. In addition, the chapter considers the full cycle of the SSC, and recommends improvements to the ONA's processes for tracking conclusions and recommendations from its continuous supervision activities. If the ONA moves towards a more data-driven, automated approach, additional expertise and specialised data skills will also be needed to enhance the SSC.

Finally, the chapter recognises the political economy and overall context in which the ONA and the SSC operate. Specifically, the ONA is breaking ground on continuous supervision in Spain and this has implications for stakeholders that have a direct impact on the SSC, or on institutions who could benefit from knowing the results of the monitoring for enhancing their own governance. The chapter therefore offers recommendations to promote the transparency, communication and co-ordination for continuous supervision. Specifically, the ONA could strengthen the transparency of its efforts by publishing the annual reports of the SSC. An audit committee with the SSC as part of its responsibility could also help to promote transparency as well as ensure input from stakeholders across government, including the Ministry of Finance, Council of Ministers and other oversight bodies. The chapter also encourages the IGAE and the ONA to enhance co-ordination and communication with key oversight institutions, in part to avoid duplication but also to demonstrate the value of the SSC as it evolves.

References

Canada Border Services Agency (2019), *Audit of Enterprise Architecture*, https://www.cbsa-asfc.gc.ca/agency-agence/reports-rapports/ae-ve/2019/ea-ae-eng.html. [5]

European Platform Undeclared Work (2016), *Data Mining for more Efficient Enforcement*. [11]

Fazekas, M., Ugale, G, & Zhao, A. (2019), *Analytics for Integrity: Data-Driven Approaches for Enhancing Corruption and Fraud Risk Assessments*, OECD, Paris, https://www.oecd.org/gov/ethics/analytics-for-integrity.pdf. [10]

Government of Spain (2019), *Royal Decree-Law 3/2019*, https://www.boe.es/diario_boe/txt.php?id=BOE-A-2019-1782. [17]

Government of Spain (2018), *Official Gazette (Boletín Oficial del Estado)*, https://www.boe.es/eli/es/o/2018/04/09/hfp371. [22]

Government of Spain (2015), *Official Gazette (Boletín Oficial del Estado)*, https://www.boe.es/buscar/act.php?id=BOE-A-2015-10566. [23]

Government of Spain (2003), *Law 47/2003, of November 26, General Budgetary*, https://www.boe.es/buscar/act.php?id=BOE-A-2003-21614&p=20201231&tn=6. [16]

IGAE (2019), *Norma Internacional de Auditoría (NIA-ES-SP) 1610: Utilización del trabajo de un experto del auditor*, https://www.igae.pap.hacienda.gob.es/sitios/igae/es-ES/Control/CFPyAP/Documents/Copia_Electr%C3%B3nica_NIA-ES-SP%201620%20%20NOTA.pdf. [26]

International Auditing and Assurance Standards Board (2013), *International Standard on Auditing (ISA) 610*, https://www.ifac.org/system/files/publications/files/ISA-610-(Revised-2013).pdf. [25]

International Budget Partnership (2019), *Open Budget Survey: Spain Country Summary*, https://www.internationalbudget.org/open-budget-survey/country-results/2019/spain. [15]

OECD (2020), *Auditing Decentralised Policies in Brazil: Collaborative and Evidence-Based Approaches for Better Outcomes*, OECD Public Governance Reviews, OECD Publishing, Paris, https://dx.doi.org/10.1787/30023307-en. [4]

OECD (2020), "Digital Government Index: 2019 results", *OECD Public Governance Policy Papers*, No. 3, OECD Publishing, Paris, https://dx.doi.org/10.1787/4de9f5bb-en. [8]

OECD (2020), *OECD Fact-Finding Interview with the Inspector General of Services for the Ministry of Finance (Inspección General de Servicios del Ministerio de la Hacienda)*. [28]

OECD (2020), *OECD Fact-finding interviews with the National Audit Office (Oficina Nacional de Auditoría, ONA)*. [2]

OECD (2019), *The Path to Becoming a Data-Driven Public Sector*, OECD Digital Government Studies, OECD Publishing, Paris, https://dx.doi.org/10.1787/059814a7-en. [9]

OECD (2014), *Spain: From Administrative Reform to Continuous Improvement*, OECD Public Governance Reviews, OECD Publishing, Paris, https://dx.doi.org/10.1787/9789264210592-en. [1]

ONA (2020), *Informe de Evaluación Supervisión Continua 2017 y 2019*. [3]

ONA (2018), *Estrategia del Sistema de Supervisión Continua (2018-2020)*. [24]

The European Confederation of Institutes of Internal Auditing (2019), *Audit Committees in the* [21]
Public Sector., https://www.eciia.eu/wp-content/uploads/2019/07/Audit-Committee-Paper-8th-
draft-15.7-disp.pdf.

The Institute of Internal Auditors (2019), *Supplemental Guidance: Unique Aspects of Auditing in* [27]
the Public Sector.

The Institute of Internal Auditors (2017), *International Professoinal Practices Framework:* [18]
Implementation Guide 2440--Disseminating Results, https://na.theiia.org/standards-
guidance/Public%20Documents/Transparency%20of%20the%20Internal%20Audit%20Report
%20in%20the%20Public%20Sector.pdf.

The Institute of Internal Auditors (2014), *Global Public Sector Insight: Independent Audit* [20]
Commitees in Public Sector Organisations, https://global.theiia.org/standards-
guidance/Public%20Documents/Independent-Audit-Committees-in-Public-Sector-
Organizations.pdf.

The Institute of Internal Auditors (2009), *Practice Advisory 2500.A1-1: Follow-up Process*, [12]
https://www.iia.nl/SiteFiles/IIA_leden/Parktijkadviezen/PA%202500A1-1.pdf.

The Institute of internal Auditors (2012), *Leading Practice: Transparency of the Internal Audit in* [19]
the Public Sector, https://na.theiia.org/standards-
guidance/Public%20Documents/Transparency%20of%20the%20Internal%20Audit%20Report
%20in%20the%20Public%20Sector.pdf.

The Institute of Internal Auditors Australia (2020), *Reporting on the Status of Audit* [14]
Recommendations, https://iia.org.au/sf_docs/default-source/technical-resources/2018-
whitepapers/iia-whitepaper_reporting-on-the-status-of-audit-recommendations.pdf?sfvrsn=2.

US Goverment Accountability Office (2021), *GAO: Duplication and Cost Savings*, [13]
https://www.gao.gov/duplication-cost-savings (accessed on 21 March 2021).

US Government Accountability Office (2017), *Organizational Transformation: A Framework for* [6]
Assessing and Improving Enterprise Architecture Management,
https://www.gao.gov/assets/gao-10-846g.pdf.

US Government Accountability Office (2004), *Information Technology Investment Management:* [7]
A Framework for Assessing and Improving Process Maturity,
https://www.gao.gov/assets/gao-04-394g.pdf.

Notes

[1] Part II, Chapter II, Organisation and Functioning of the state institutional public sector. Article 81.2 requires public administrations to establish a system of continuous supervision of their dependent entities, justifying the reasons for their existence and financial sustainability and include proposals to maintain, transform or dissolve the entity. Article 84 defines the categories of public sector entities in scope for continuous supervision and efficiency control reviews while Article 85 defines the roles and responsibilities of the *Hacienda*, the IGAE and the ministerial inspection units.

[2] General data about public entities from INVESPE/INVENTE, also developed and maintained by the IGAE, is transmitted to "El Cubo" using automated processes.

[3] OECD (2020[8]), "Digital Government Index: 2019 results", *OECD Public Governance Policy Papers*, No. 3. Spain was ranked seventh overall of 33 countries and fourth on the *digital by design*, *data-driven public sector* and *proactiveness* dimensions.

[4] The OBS assesses the "online availability, timeliness, and comprehensiveness of eight key budget documents using 109 equally weighted indicators and scores each country on a scale of 0 to 100" (International Budget Partnership, 2019[15]).

[5] Box 8.1 Audit, evaluation and inspection in the context of the Spanish control framework.

[6] Article 85 Effectiveness control and continuous supervision.

[7] Interview with the Gabinete Técnico, Tribunal de Cuentas, December 2020.